PRENTICE-HALL

Foundations of Cultural Geography Series

PHILIP L. WAGNER, Editor

RICHARD E. DAHLBERG, Series Cartographer

* In Prentice-Hall's Foundations of Economic Geography Series, also.

Foundations of Cultural Geography Series

RICHARD E. DAHLBERG, *Series Cartographer*

Geography of Religions

David E. Sopher

Syracuse University

PRENTICE-HALL, INC., Englewood Cliffs, N.J.

© 1967 by Prentice-Hall, Inc.
   Englewood Cliffs, N.J.

Library of Congress Catalog Card No.: 67-13357

Current printing (last number):
10 9 8 7 6 5 4 3 2 1

PRENTICE-HALL INTERNATIONAL, INC., London
PRENTICE-HALL OF AUSTRALIA, PTY. LTD., Sydney
PRENTICE-HALL OF CANADA, LTD., Toronto
PRENTICE-HALL OF INDIA PRIVATE LTD., New Delhi
PRENTICE-HALL OF JAPAN, INC., Tokyo

Foundations of Cultural Geography Series

The title of this series, Foundations of Cultural Geography, represents its purpose well. Our huge and highly variegated store of knowledge about the ways that humans occupy and use their world becomes most meaningful when studied in the light of certain basic questions. Original studies of such basic questions make up this series of books by leading scholars in the field.

The authors of the series report and evaluate current thought centered on the questions: How do widely different systems of ideas and practice influence what people do to recreate and utilize their habitats? How do such systems of thought and habitat spread and evolve? How do human efforts actually change environments, and with what effects?

These questions are approached comparatively, respecting the great range of choice and experience available to mankind. They are treated historically as well, to trace and interpret and assess what man has done at various times and places. They are studied functionally, too, and whatever controlling processes and relationships they may reveal are sought.

Diverse tastes and talents govern the authors' attack on these problems. One deals with religion as a system of ideas both influencing and reflecting environmental conditions. Another evaluates the role of belief and custom in reshaping plant and animal species to human purposes. Some consider the use and meaning of human creations, like houses or cities, in geographic context; others treat of the subtle and complex relationships with nature found in agricultural systems of many sorts. One author looks at an entire country as a culturally-shaped environment; another analyzes the mechanics of the spread of customs and beliefs in space. All work toward an understanding of the same key problems. We invite the reader to participate actively in the critical rethinking by which scholarship moves forward.

PHILIP L. WAGNER

v

to Valerie and Jonathan

Preface

Substantive and methodological writing that deals with religion within the field of geography is small in bulk and scattered among publications in several languages. Although geographers have long recognized that religious ideas and organization may play an important role in the way man occupies and shapes the land, important geographic studies focusing on this theme only recently have begun to appear. This little book, building on some of these pioneer studies, which are cited in their appropriate places in the text, is hardly more than a map of a frontier territory with some indications where its boundaries may lie. In scanning the terrain, I have been constantly aware of the vast and scarcely exploited material resources represented by the literature on religion—its phenomenology, its history, its sociology. I can only regret that my own knowledge of these resources is so limited that it precludes all but the barest notations concerning them in this survey.

I am deeply indebted to the editor of the series, Professor Philip Wagner, and to my colleagues Professor Isma'il al Faruqi and Professor Donald Meinig for stimulating discussion, discerning comment, and critical reading of all or part of the manuscript. I am grateful to Professor Richard Dahlberg, John Fonda, and the Department of Geography, Syracuse University, for generous assistance in the design and preparation of the maps. I am unboundedly thankful to my wife, Terry, who encouraged me, contributed ideas and critical comment, and accomplished the impossible by translating innumerable pages of my handwriting into typescript.

Grateful acknowledgment is also extended to the following: Oxford University Press, for permission to reproduce copyrighted map material in Figure 1; University of Utah Press, for permission to adapt a copyrighted photograph in Figure 2(A); the Department of Geography, University of Chicago, for permission to use Goode's Map No. 101HC and Goode's Homolosine Projection, copyright by The University of Chicago, for the base map in figures 5 and 6; Dr. Helen Wallis, Map Room, British Museum, for assistance in obtaining a copy of Dr. Hume's map, Figure 11; Messrs. Darton, Longman & Todd, Ltd., for permission to adapt copyrighted map material in figures 12 and 13.

DAVID E. SOPHER

The ambiguous and fascinating interplay of symbolic values with environment, which is the topic of Dr. Sopher's pioneering study, makes a fitting subject to introduce the series. As he shows, religious customs, even when they mirror times and places far away, profoundly influence the fate and fortunes of societies and the forms of landscape. Most of the great themes of cultural geography are encountered constantly in his study, and it effectively expresses the spirit of the discipline.

PHILIP L. WAGNER

Contents

CHAPTER 1
of religion
the geographic study

Cultural geography is concerned with man, not as an individual, but as a sharer and bearer of culture. Its particular concern is with two kinds of relationships: the interaction between a culture and its complex earth environment, and the spatial interaction among different cultures. The geography of religion investigates these relationships, concentrating its attention on the religious component in culture.

Geography cannot deal with the personal religious experience, which is to some the core of religion. But religion has been defined as "a system of faith and worship; . . . a body of institutionalized sacred beliefs, observances, and social practices." [1] Geography *can* study organized religious systems and culturally molded and institutionalized religious behavior.

There are other difficulties in the geographic study of religious phenomena. Bias in the historical and scholarly record is a pervasive problem. However, the land provides a record of religion that is subject to geographic scrutiny and can be used at times to check the accuracy of questionable assertions. A second difficulty concerns behavioral norms. Large segments of a society may deviate from the observances and social practices prescribed by their nominal religion. A geography of religions should be concerned primarily with modal behavior, but areal variation in departures from religious norms often cannot be ascertained. As a Christian scholar has noted, there is a world of difference between "being religious" and "having a religion." Almost all mankind can be said to have a religion,[2] and it is this condition that can be the object of geographic study.

Qualified in these ways, religion is treated here within the framework of

[1] *Webster's Third New International Dictionary* (Springfield, Mass.: G. & C. Merriam Company, 1961).

[2] A. C. Bouquet, *Comparative Religion*, 6th ed. (Baltimore: Penguin Books, Inc., 1962), p. 13. See also J. Paul Williams, "The Nature of Religion," *Journal for the Scientific Study of Religion*, II (1962), 3-14.

four cultural geographic themes. Considered in turn are (1) the significance of the environmental setting for the evolution of religious systems and particular religious institutions; (2) the way religious systems and institutions modify their environment; (3) the different ways whereby religious systems occupy and organize segments of earth space; (4) the geographic distribution of religions and the way religious systems spread and interact with each other.

Labeling of Religious Systems

We must first select, sort, and classify the data of religion within a suitable geographic framework, but the labeling of religious systems itself presents a number of difficulties. The Western concept of a formal religious system, having as its essence a fixed relationship between man and God, does not fit the Oriental religious systems. One cannot speak of people in the Oriental world as having a religion in the exact way one can identify persons as Christians or Muslims. Sharp confessional boundaries separate Christian, Muslim, and Jew. Their religions, grouped for convenience as the Western Old World religions, are exclusivist, having traditionally regarded other religions as false, and are thus distinguished from the religions prevailing over much of southern and eastern Asia where the boundaries of adherence are blurred or overlap.[3]

While it is of geographical importance that the Western Old World religions are exclusivist in contrast to the Oriental religions, it is less important that the former happen to be monotheisms, the latter not. The theological and philosophical content of religions cannot alone provide an adequate basis for geographical analysis.

There is a question whether one can usefully treat even the exclusivist religions as single systems. Christianity, in recent centuries, has scarcely been one system. The current ecumenizing trend is changing the picture, but the actual patterns of organization and the nature of interrelationships among different Christian populations make it preferable to speak of Christianity as a grouping of several historically related but relatively independent subsystems, with some common features. One of these features is the attitude of exclusivism. Within Protestantism, exclusivism is carried right through to sects that are the product of several successive stages of fission. The division of Islam into Shia and Sunni communities is of a different order and has not resulted in the separation of the Islamic community into two self-sufficient and mutually exclusive parts. On the other hand, both Islam and Christianity have given rise to derivative but strongly idiosyncratic forms, such as the Druze and Mormon religions, not fully accepted by the parent system.

Even if the effects of secularism and Communism are not taken into account, the religions of societies in the Far East and India are not easily labeled. Only in a small part of the Oriental world, the Theravada Buddhist countries of southern Asia and until recently the Lamaist lands of Tibet and Mongolia, have Buddhist institutions provided an important integrating element in society, so that we can speak safely of their popu-

[3] See, e.g., Werner Cohn, "Is Religion Universal? Problems of Definition," *Journal for the Scientific Study of Religion*, II (1962), 25-33. Cohn argues that "religion" in the Western sense is an exclusively Western phenomenon.

lations as Buddhist. In other societies apparently permeated by Buddhism, the monastic population—the only truly Buddhist society—must be distinguished from both lay supporters and nonadherents. Supporters of Buddhist institutions exhibit a wide spectrum of belief and in many cases are not even exclusively committed to Buddhism.

In Buddhist China of the seventh and eighth centuries and in India around the beginning of the Christian Era, when Buddhism was ascendant, the supporting public probably comprised only a fraction of the total non-clerical population. In Japan, where Buddhism has had more lasting success than in China, the larger part of the population must be described as having dual religious affiliation; enthusiastic Japanese Buddhists also may be practicing Shintoists, and vice versa. In China, Korea, and Vietnam, where Buddhist institutions have had less vitality than in Japan, few of the non-clerical population are in any sense exclusively Buddhist. As a result, estimates of Buddhist population in China in the pre-Communist period vary enormously. Most Chinese have multiple associations with different forms of religious belief and ritual. Except for a few totally dedicated Buddhists, together with small numbers of Muslims and Christians, the Chinese pre-Communist population subscribed to the Chinese religious complex, an uneven and regionally differentiated mixture of elements and rituals of Buddhism, Confucianism, Taoism, and various folk religions.

The comparable Indian religious complex, equally unorganized, containing more diverse components, and more differentiated regionally, is called Hinduism, a designation meaning simply "the Indian religious system." Unfortunately, no such conventional term is in use for the other Oriental ethnic religious mixtures prevalent in China, Korea, Japan, and Vietnam.[4]

Hinduism is a highly incorporative religious system. One finds believing polytheists and monotheists, as well as certain kinds of atheists among Hindus, but the identity of any of these as Hindus is never in question. Hindus find the exclusive attitudes of Christianity and Islam hard to understand and accept, while their own apparently unlimited eclecticism is incomprehensible to many Westerners. A Hindu can assert that all religious human beings are in fact Hindus, whether or not they know or desire it.[5]

Religious systems like Hinduism, which accommodate divergent forms of belief, tend to absorb and incorporate large numbers of sects. Even a distinct religious system like Jainism seems almost to have been absorbed as one more Hindu sect. Perhaps only where the trait of Western exclusivism arises in a sect of Hindu derivation, as in Sikhism, does a fairly independent system develop in India.

Another problem in labeling for geographic purposes arises today from the dozens of new religions, sects, cults, and churches. Most are found among small, technologically backward ethnic groups, members until recently of nonliterate societies, suddenly brought into contact with an overwhelming alien civilization, usually the European one. Some of these

[4] "Chinese Universalism" has currency, especially in Europe, as a designation for the non-Buddhist components of the Chinese ethnic religious system.
[5] Moses Jung, Swami Nikhilananda, and Herbert W. Schneider, eds., *Relations Among Religions Today: a Handbook of Policies and Principles* (Leiden: E. J. Brill, 1963), p. 72.

new minor systems are distinct religions, such as the Peyote religion of American Indian communities in the United States and the Cargo Cults of Melanesia, while some have affiliation with a major religion. Among many of the hundreds of native African churches, the tie to Christianity is a tenuous one, while a number of them are explicitly non-Christian.

Geographic Characteristics of Religious Systems

Religious systems may be distinguished by several spatial and ecological characteristics. Features relevant for our purposes are (a) distribution, i.e., both geographic pattern and social extent; (b) structure in space, the machinery whereby a religious system organizes all its adherents; and (c) the means used by a system to grow numerically and territorially.

The religions of the majority of the world's population can be separated into two broad groups: those that are strongly ethnic in outlook and those that are universalizing. A number of religious systems that neither of these designations fits very well may be called segmental. Religious systems having an ethnic character vary greatly in the size and geographical extent of the adherent population, making a further subdivision, although necessarily an imprecise one, desirable. It is convenient to distinguish three ethnic subgroups: (1) simple ethnic or tribal systems; [6] (2) compound ethnic or national systems; and (3) complex ethnic systems associated with a major civilization.

This arrangement into groups is not to be thought of as a typing of religious systems. It recognizes certain strong and usually persistent patterns in the relationship of a given religious system to the world outside it.

ETHNIC RELIGIOUS SYSTEMS. Simple ethnic (tribal) religious systems are found today among societies which are usually small in population, which have only recently adopted a system of writing, are culturally homogeneous, not highly differentiated spatially, and are fairly closely bound to place or kin-group. Usually, their religious practices are directly related to the nature of their physical environment and the way they exploit it. These religions have sometimes been grouped under the term "animism," describing religions in which the central feature is the belief in and worship of nature spirits. But animism is not a single religious system with a sense of community, although adjacent simple ethnic religions may have many common elements. Ritual head-hunting occurs among many tribal societies in Southeast Asia and South America, and certain shamanistic ritual forms have an almost uninterrupted distribution among Arctic tribes of both the Old and the New World. The common possession of these religious traits has not engendered a feeling of community among such tribes. Maintaining their separate identity, they sometimes reinforce this separateness by accentuating quite minor differences in religious practice. However, in ancient Greece and probably among the Hebrews under the patriarchs, a partial integration of tribal

[6] "Simple ethnic" seems preferable to "tribal" because many tribal societies do adhere to one of the larger ethnic or universalizing systems. The content—thought, values, emotional power, ritual—of a "simple ethnic" religion may, of course, be far from simple.

religious systems did occur. This was the amphictyony, an association of neighboring or related tribes observing feasts in common and bound to protect a common religious center.

Religions in this group number at least several hundred and include a few, such as the Hopi and Navajo religions, found in the United States. Far from being geographically negligible (Fig. 6), their total population is today about 150 million, spread, often thinly, over several million square miles of the earth's surface. Many hundreds more of these religions have been eliminated or severely reduced within the past century by the advance of Christianity and Islam.

Millennia earlier, at the dawn of civilization, simple ethnic religious systems began to be replaced by compound ethnic systems. A compound ethnic religious system, one that is peculiar to a nation or state, reflects the complexity of economic and political organization found among its followers. Compound ethnic systems are generally associated with societies that at least have written legal and religious codes and economic specialization of the order involved in the genesis of towns. Like the religion of tribal societies, a compound ethnic religion has strong ties to a particular place and people. It is almost exclusively the religion of a country or a culturally homogeneous people, and an outsider enters the system only through a process of naturalization or acculturation—by coming to be of the land or of the people.

Most of these systems are ancient ones, now defunct and known only from history. Shinto, the indigenous Japanese religion, is a living example. Others were the ancient Mayan religious system; the combined cults of the Nile, the Sun, and other deities that comprised the religious system of ancient Egypt; the religion of the Hebrew states of Judah and Israel in the first half of the first millennium before the Christian Era; and a number of local cults in the city-states of the eastern Mediterranean in antiquity.

Although the Mediterranean cults did share certain features such as the worship of the Great Goddess, they were usually associated with a particular town or district. In Hellenic and Roman times, some of them were taken by adherents to new locations, where, in the form of mystery religions, they attracted a following, even though the religion or cult continued to have a strong association with its place of origin. Judaism, which has a marked ethnic character, also spread in this way.

In spite of its wide dispersion, Judaism must be considered an ethnic religious system because its institutions and practices are closely tied to the land of its origin. Judaism is simply the religion of the community that shares the tradition of these ties to a particular place. Its theology, ethic, and ritual make a unique combination which preserves the tradition and so preserves the distinctive identity of the community. The ethnic character of Judaism can be demonstrated in many ways, but perhaps in none more clearly than by noting that while Christians distinguish between themselves and the pagan or heathen, and the Muslims between themselves and the *kāfir*, or unbeliever, the popular Jewish antithesis is between Jew and *goi*, that is, "gentile," a word which has the meaning of "ethnic group." The distinction is thus between Jews and other ethnic groups.

The complex systems of India and China are larger ethnic religious systems integrating many local cults that are nevertheless encouraged to flourish. The Chinese religious complex traditionally contained an official cult which served as an important space-integrating agent. Rites symbolizing the national needs were performed by government officers. Religion thus came to be a branch of government. The official cult gave strong national expression to a peculiarly Chinese mixture of diverse religious institutions, including the highly localized practices associated with reverence for ancestors. The Korean and Vietnamese religions were much like this, partly because of Chinese influence, but each was built around a separate ethnos, thus giving the Koreans and Vietnamese an early national identity distinct from that of the Chinese.

The largest and most elaborate of these ethnic systems is Hinduism. Hinduism may seem to be universal because of its extraordinary eclecticism regarding religious content, but its religious content cannot be separated effectively from the caste society of India, the social order to which Hinduism is bound and which gives it its ethnic character.

Hinduism's ties to place are expressed in ancient concepts of the sanctity of the Indian space: sacred Ganges, sacred cities, Brahmavarta, "the land of the Brahmans." At a lower level, Hinduism is even more closely tied to place and kin-group by the nature of caste, an exclusive social unit, usually of restricted territorial extent, which has a traditional functional responsibility within the society of a particular territory. The obligation to discharge this responsibility, together with other caste-specific patterns of social behavior and ritual, constitutes the *dharma* or religion of a caste. Each caste has its own *dharma*, but there are common threads running through individual caste codes. Hinduism does provide world-renouncing avenues of escape from the rigid caste bonds of kin and place, but these are practicable for a small minority only.[7]

Although elements of this place-bound Indian religious system appear in the early civilization of Southeast Asia, Hinduism cannot be considered a universalizing system. Hindu elements often spread together with Buddhism, a truly universalizing system. A small number of Hindu merchants and literati, representing a narrow but influential selection of the total population, may have migrated, and through their contacts, selected elements of the Hindu complex may have been widely diffused. We know of no organized proselytizing, the basic Hindu caste structure was not transferred abroad, and no identifying links were maintained with India or with other "Hinduized" populations like those connecting East Asian Buddhists to the Buddhist hearth in India. After 1200, Theravada Buddhism and Islam began to create new religious integrations in Southeast Asia. Until then, religious elements of Indian origin blended with local religions of simple structure to form compound ethnic religious systems like those of East Asia.

The Oriental religious complexes can be considered as integrated religious systems because they are made up of interdependent elements. Each Hindu caste's *dharma* is confined to the concerns of that caste, but any performance of the *dharma* depends on the like performance of their

[7] Only if Hinduism is restricted to mean those elements that go beyond caste can it be treated as a "world religion" (i.e., a universalizing system), as it is by Arnold Toynbee, *A Study of History* (London and New York: Oxford University press, 1934-62, twelve volumes), and more recently by William H. McNeill, *The Rise of the West* (Chicago: University of Chicago Press, 1963).

dharma by all other castes. In imperial China, the official cult, the temples of the folk religions with their local nature deities, and the domestic rites in honor of the ancestors all represented religious specializations, each of which formed an interdependent part of the whole. An ostensibly independent system like Buddhism, having failed to become dominant, was obliged to accept an interdependent role within a society subscribing to the Chinese religious system. The interdependence of Buddhism and local ethnic religions is illustrated in Japan, where most Japanese are married by a Shinto priest but at death are cremated according to Buddhist practice. This pattern of interdependence does not normally govern relations with those independent Western Old World religions or autonomous tribal religions found among the major Oriental ethnic systems.

Precisely because of their ethnicity, all these ethnically oriented religions have limited means of extension, which in turn affects their distribution. Apart from natural growth and migration, ethnic systems may expand gradually along their territorial margins as a result of intensive contact with other religious systems, particularly the simple tribal ones. This is the process of contact conversion, in which the usual agents of conversion are entire social groups, and conversion is part of a broad acculturative process. Conversion, as used here, does not necessarily resemble the Christian or Muslim process. It may be a gradual transition, for conversion to an ethnic religious system brings with it not so much a new religious belief as it does a whole new ethnos.

In India, this process has long been at work. It still draws non-Hindu tribal folk like the Bhils, Gonds, and Santals of the Middle Indian jungle lands into the socio-religious fold of Hinduism. The Chinese religious complex has also progressively enlarged its borders by absorbing the simple religious organisms of China's barbarian neighbors. Judaism, too, has occasionally expanded geographically in this way, notably in Arabia in the centuries before Islam appeared. Religions of this kind have no mechanism for rapidly acquiring new members in large numbers. Hinduism in its modern eclectic garb has developed missions, but on a very minor scale. Their object has usually been to hasten the acculturative process among tribal folk or to win back Hindus converted to Christianity or Islam. Ethnic religious systems appear rather static, despite the mobility of some communities expressed in the widespread diasporas or partial diasporas of Jews, Hindus, and Chinese.

UNIVERSALIZING RELIGIOUS SYSTEMS.   Universalizing religious systems are those which (a) are considered by their adherents to be proper to all mankind, (b) have mechanisms to facilitate their transmittal, (c) have at some time successfully broken through the restrictions of a special relationship to place or particular social group, and (d) have been established as dominant religions at least on a regional scale.[8]

Buddhism, Christianity, and Islam—in chronological order—are the three major universalizing systems. Universalizing religions are generally "religions of revelation," although these almost always begin as revelations in a closed ethnic field. The message of Jesus Christ was communi-

[8] The term "universalizing" is used in order not to confuse the Hindu and Chinese systems with Buddhism, Christianity, and Islam, all five being sometimes called "universal" or "world" religions.

cated specifically to the Jews, that of Muhammad circulated chiefly among the Arabs of Central Arabia, at least during much of the prophet's career. The Arabs remained the "chosen people" of Islam for about a century, non-Arab converts to Islam being treated as second-class citizens. These revelations, elaborated as messages to all humanity, became the basis of universalizing systems through the success of their extranational appeal.

Techniques such as simple conversion and missionary endeavor permit the rapid expansion of universalizing systems. Admission to the community of believers can come after slight conditioning, in contrast to the long process of acculturation and absorption into the ethnic systems. In Buddhism, there are no formalities of admission or expulsion; adherence is a simple voluntary act. In the case of Islam, adherence is demonstrated by the recital of a formula. The rites of baptism and communion constitute admission into most Christian communities. These simple acts are the symbols of a dramatic exchange, which the term "conversion" connotes.

Universalizing systems do not always have well-developed missionary institutions. Islam is notably deficient in this respect. But all of them seek to impart their message to the widest possible audience, so that proselytizing zeal often becomes a moral obligation for members of the religious community. In Islam and Christianity, proselytizing fervor has been reinforced by the belief in the falsity of all other systems and the wish to eliminate them.

The evolution of universalizing religious systems in western Asia began before the appearance of Christianity. The Hebrew prophets expressed universalizing themes, but the religious system could not implement them; the brief proselytizing of the Hellenic period was done by partly de-ethnicized Jewish communities through contact conversion in a receptive milieu. A more explicitly universalizing movement was the religion preached by Zoroaster in Persia in the sixth century B.C. Failing to expand beyond the Persian territory, it became a hierarchical official religion without mass popularity. Displaced by the rise and spread of Islam, Zoroastrianism survives chiefly in India, where it has been for centuries a quasi-ethnic religious system.

Zoroastrian universalist elements appeared in the new religion of Mithras, evolving in Asia Minor in the first century B.C., after the Roman Conquest. Its priestless brotherhood of the faithful and its masculine emphasis made it popular in the Roman army. It was a rival of early Christianity and quite as widely dispersed; archaeological remains of this ancient universalizing system have been found from Persia to the borders of Scotland. The eastern Roman provinces provided a favorable situation for the spread of ethnic cults. Originally place-bound cults like those of Isis and Cybele became fashionable and popular; and as mystery religions actively attracting initiates of different cultures with the message of personal salvation and eternal life, they were virtually universalizing systems.

The success of universalizing systems like Christianity and Buddhism provided a model for much subsequent religious development, although only Islam achieved a like success.[9] In the third century A.D., Manichae-

[9] This excludes Marxism which may be treated as a universalizing quasi-religious system; see Chapter 6.

ism acquired a following on the Mesopotamian margins of the Roman Empire, where it came into conflict with exclusivist Christianity. Subsequently it spread among the pastoralists and oasis dwellers of Turkic Central Asia, where it was ultimately overcome by Islam, disappearing in the fourteenth century.

More recently, new types of religious universalism have arisen from the major religious systems as reforming and transcending movements. Two examples are the related syncretistic movements of the Bahai and Babi which developed out of Islam in nineteenth century Persia and acquired an international following.

The universality of Christianity and Buddhism and, to a lesser extent, of Islam, has been continually threatened by local ethnicizing processes, particularly in their spatial organization. At an early date, the world Christian community experienced a fourfold regional division corresponding approximately to the pattern of civilizations at the time. The domain of the Roman Catholic Church corresponded to that of Latin civilization, the Byzantine Church dominated the Hellenic area, the Monophysite Christian community occupied the Hellenicized Middle East (Syria, Armenia, Egypt), while the Nestorian Church spread into Mesopotamia and the extra-Roman Asiatic world. As late as 1200, the Nestorian and Monophysite churches had as many followers as the two European Christian subsystems,[10] but they became increasingly isolated after Islam won mass acceptance. These Middle Eastern subsystems have survived as separate churches with a marked ethnic character, expressed among other ways in distinct liturgical languages. Because of its isolation from Roman ecumenical efforts, the best maintained of these ethnicized Christian subsystems today is the Ethiopian Orthodox Church, a derivative of Monophysite Christianity.

The division of Christianity into virtually independent and often mutually antagonistic churches, epitomized by the Reformation and stimulated by it, is to some extent a rejection of the universalizing aims of the system.[11] Although the Roman Church since the Reformation has not experienced a comparable organizational split, it has not entirely succeeded in overcoming ethnicizing trends. The Spanish and Portuguese monarchs' virtually independent administration of the Church in their overseas territories—the Real Patronato (royal patronage)—was a quasi-national organizational development. More than one truly ethnic splinter church has broken off from Rome in this century. One is the nationalist Filipino church, the Aglipayan Independent Church of the Philippines. Established in 1902 in protest against the dominance of foreign Catholic clergy in the Philippines, it now embraces about 5 per cent of the Philippine population, of which 83 per cent continue to belong to the Roman Catholic Church.

Such subsystems of the universalizing religions may acquire an increasingly ethnic character, as the Ethiopian church did, under conditions of continuing geographic isolation and loss of internal dynamism.

---

[10] Toynbee, op. cit., Vol. 2, pp. 360-69.

[11] Toynbee, A Study of History, Vol. 4, p. 222, speaks of the "Protestant enormity" of such "parochial" established churches as the Church of England, an independent ethnically organized Christian subsystem.

But some Christian subsystems organized originally on a national basis, like the Anglican Church (the Church of England and its offshoots), do carry on missionary activity. Moreover, such ethnicized bodies as the Independent Church of the Philippines and the Church of England, together with its separate nationalist offshoot, the Protestant Episcopal Church in the United States, have not been absolutely exclusivist but have acknowledged and have recently fostered links with other Christian subsystems.

In a broad sense, all the universalizing religions, even the most successful, have acquired a certain ethnic character vis-à-vis other religious systems, especially as cultural horizons have widened to include the whole world. Islam, having overcome an initial ethnicizing tendency represented by such features as special mosques for different tribes in its early decades, is seen today by most non-Muslims as having an ineradicably Arabic appearance that conceals what universality of appeal it may have. Christianity has also acquired an ethnic identity in some lands. In recent decades it has had to face the fact that in much of Asia and Africa it is marked as "the white man's religion." This image of an ethnicizing rather than a universalizing Christianity is consciously conveyed by those Protestant churches in South Africa and the American South which segregate the organized Christian community into mutually exclusive ethnic components, White and Negro.[12] Aware that Christianity is threatened by this ethnic label, the Catholic Church is presently engaged in a partial de-Europeanization of the higher ranks of church officers.

Being separately organized, the Catholic, Eastern Orthodox, and Protestant churches, like the separate branches of Buddhism, normally operate as independent universalizing systems. Early in Christian history, the independent Nestorian subsystem, although regarded as heretical by Rome and Byzantium, expended considerable proselytizing effort in much of western and central Asia. Other universalizing subsystems of Christianity, including some which have been out of favor with the longer established churches, have appeared since then. The unusual history of the Mormon Church (Church of Jesus Christ of Latter-Day Saints) provides a recent illustration. Persecuted, exiled, isolated, tending for a time to become a new ethnic religion but soon recovering and developing vigorous missionary institutions, it is today a virtually independent universalizing religious system within the tenuous structure of Protestant Christianity.[13]

SEGMENTAL RELIGIOUS SYSTEMS. A segmental religious system, occupying only a part of a larger social framework, has no universalizing aspirations or has ceased to have them. Some segmental systems are limited to a stratal distribution as the dominant religion of a particular social class, while others, established as dominants within particular areas, tend to create neoethnic regional differentiation.

[12] The universality of Mormonism is also restricted in fact, Negroes being excluded from priesthood in the Mormon religion.
[13] Various sides of the question whether Mormons are operationally Protestants or even Christians are presented in William J. Whalen, *The Latter-Day Saints in the Modern Day World* (New York: The John Day Company, Inc., 1964), pp. 108-17. Mormons do not consider themselves Protestants.

Friction-generated nativistic or messianic religions like the Cargo Cults of Melanesia are segmental in the sense that they arise in the interstices between a European cultural overlay and the traditional culture system. These religions may employ some of the practices and phraseology of the major universalizing religions, but they are never universalizing themselves precisely because they make a significant ethnic differentiation between their potential audience and others, who are usually the Whites. But these new religions often cut across old tribal boundaries and are to that extent neoethnic. Pan-Indianism is a vital part of the appeal and function of the Native American (Peyote) Church; it brings together in an original way the remnants of the ethnically diverse Indian population, and at the same time bases itself on the reality of a gulf between Indian and White.[14]

The contact of European culture with the weakly organized religious systems of the Orient has also helped to spawn new segmental religions such as the Cao Dai religion in South Vietnam, the Chondo-kyo religion in Korea, and idiosyncratic Buddhist sects like the semipolitical Soka Gakkai in Japan. Some new religions claim to belong to a major universalizing system, as some of the native African churches do, but they are actually independent. The neo-Buddhists among the depressed classes in India and the Black Muslims in the United States are other instances of this phenomenon.

In certain circumstances, such new religious growths may in time become more closely tied to the larger systems with which they claim relationship. In South Africa, the Congo, and West Africa, there is a spectrum of splinter churches which spreads across the boundary of acceptance of and by Christianity. The missions used to denounce such churches, claiming to be Christian, as heretical and regarded them as a "failure of the missions." Lately, however, some of the missions have adopted the view that these nativistic churches testify to the successful penetration of Christianity and to its universality.[15]

Offshoots that become almost detached from a parent universalizing system appear as segmental systems, often with neoethnic tendencies. The Druze religious system is an example of this. Although a subsystem of Islam, it no longer makes converts or permits apostasy, forming a closed ethnic community with its own territorial base in southwestern Syria. Had the Mormon settlements in Utah been isolated for a longer period, and had Mormonism not developed proselytizing institutions, a striking analogy to the Druze situation might have developed.

Another type of segmental religion is the unsuccessful universalizing religion that may survive as the religion of one segment of a society. The Bahai and Brahmo Samaj movements may be noted as new religions that have almost reached this point. Jainism, a contemporary of Bud-

[14] For absorbing accounts of these and other new nativistic religions and the phenomenon of "prophet-salvation" movements among peoples of simple ethnic religions, see Vittorio Lanternari, *The Religion of the Oppressed: a Study of Modern Messianic Cults*, trans. Lisa Sergio (New York: Alfred A. Knopf, Inc., 1963) and G. Guariglia, *Prophetismus und Heilserwartungsbewegungen als völkerkundliches und religionsgeschichtliches Problem*, Wiener Beiträge zur Kulturgeschichte und Linguistik, XIII (Horn-Wien: Berger, 1959).

[15] Lanternari, *op. cit.*, p. 58.

dhism, had only limited success within India and is now confined as a stratal religion to a predominantly middle class urban population in western India. One sect emphasizes the stratal character of the Jain system by automatically excluding cultivators, regarding the work of agriculture as polluting because it involves the destruction of minute animal life. Sikhism, on the other hand, found its adherents principally in the middle level agrarian class of Punjabi Jats. Although it retains its universalizing intentions, it has never successfully escaped its Punjabi associations and remains a segmental religion with an increasingly neoethnic character. Some American Protestant denominations, especially smaller sects like the Amish, have a similar segmental character within American society, operating within it as fairly independent and partially closed subsystems.

Official state cults represent another kind of stratal religion, especially when observance of the cult is the exclusive prerogative of a ruling class. This was the character of the Roman imperial religion of Divine Caesar and the goddess Roma and the later cult of the sun god, Sol Invictus. Official cults formed stratal components in the religions of ancient Egypt and Confucian China.

A word should be said here about religions of very limited extent. Quite apart from the great range in belief and practice among people who are members of some larger religious community, there have been many "idiosyncratic" religions, private and personal beliefs and forms of worship subscribed to by individuals and small organized groups. This includes the beliefs of individual heretics, atheists, and various kinds of agnostics who are not organized as communities.

The great "religions of revelation" have all started as idiosyncratic religions, confined at first to a handful of faithful. No doubt many other religions claiming revelation have never developed beyond this stage and have ultimately disappeared.

Some idiosyncratic religions have been the inspiration or invention of rulers and other influential persons. Accepted perfunctorily by a coterie for a time, they have generally failed to survive their authors. Examples of the genre are the Egyptian Pharaoh Ikhnaton's attempt to create a revolutionary state religion of monotheism; the Emperor Julian's reorganization of paganism in the fourth century as a reaction to Christianity; the syncretistic Din-i-Ilahi (Divine Religion) which was the bold conception of the Mogul emperor Akbar, faced with the problem of keeping the peace among his subjects of different faiths; and Robespierre's "Cult of the Supreme Being and of Nature," promulgated as a national religion during the French Revolution.

The variety of religious systems just outlined is often concealed by statistics that deal only with the larger ones. Table 1 is an attempt to present the total world picture. Data were obtained from a number of sources, but no adjustment of the figures has been made to suggest actual observance rather than nominal affiliation within a religious tradition. The raw data were not of uniform date and have therefore been adjusted to a total world population of three billion, equivalent to the condition in

Table 1. Religions of the World (1963)

(All population figures in millions)

Religion	Population		
Ethnic religious systems			1,174
Simple (tribal) [a]		150	
Judaism		13	
Shinto		35	
Vietnamese and Korean religions		36	
Chinese religion		540 ?	
Hinduism		400	
Universalizing religious systems			1,557
Buddhism		240	
Theravada	65		
Mahayana [b]	175 ?		
Christianity		897	
Catholic	530		
Protestant	260		
Lutheran	70		
Presbyterian and Calvinist	45		
Baptist	40		
Anglican [c]	30		
Methodist	30		
Other [d]	45		
Eastern	107		
Russian Orthodox (USSR)	50 ?		
Other Orthodox and Eastern [e]	57		
Islam [f]		420	
Segmental religious systems			14
Sikhism		7.5	
Cao Dai, Chondo-kyo, etc.		4.5	
Jainism		2	
Minor religions and no religious affiliation [g]			255
TOTAL			3,000

[a] Includes numerous new nativistic and millennarian religions.

[b] Estimate for China based on prewar data of dubious reliability: 100 million.

[c] The conventional designation "Protestant" is rejected by many members of the churches of the Anglican Communion.

[d] Includes Mormons, etc.

[e] Includes Coptic, Armenian, Ethiopian, and Malabar Christian churches.

[f] Shia and derivative sects (Druzes, etc.) estimated to be about 10 per cent of total Muslim population.

[g] Mainly descendants of population of Christian tradition in Western Europe and the Soviet Union.

mid-1963. The figures presented here are, for the most part, gross estimates.[16]

[16] It is difficult to get reliable statistics of precise religious affiliation in countries like the United States, where religion has come to be considered not a proper subject for official census enumeration. See, e.g., William Petersen, "Religious Statistics in the United States," *Journal for the Scientific Study of Religion*, I (1962), 165-78; W. Zelinsky, "An Approach to the Religious Geography of the United States: Patterns of Church Membership in 1952," *Annals*, Association of American Geographers, LI (1961), 141-44.

CHAPTER 2 *religious systems— the geographic base*

Geography can help to determine to what extent religious systems or their component elements are an expression of ecological circumstances.[1] Careful use of geographical and historical data is needed in order to avoid what Erich Isaac calls the "etiological fallacy." [2] This has happened when "geography" has been invoked inappropriately in the formulation of environmentalist and functionalist generalizations about the origin of religions and religious practices.

For example, the sanctity of the Ganges in Hindu belief is sometimes explained in this way: the river is of great economic importance to the people along its banks and so earns respect, formalized as worship. This seems plausible, and there is the analogue of the life-giving Nile as sacred river. However, the sanctity of the Ganges extends from source to mouth and is as strong in relatively inaccessible regions as it is in densely populated ones. Nor is the Ganges uniquely sacred. Almost the same level of sanctity is ascribed locally to other large Indian rivers that, like the sacred Narbada, may be of little economic use.

The sanctity of the Ganges, Narbada, Kaveri, and other Indian rivers is not associated with a perception of the river as part of a larger ecological system. In India, flowing water is purifying.[3] The extraordinary opportunities for the elimination of pollution provided by the Ganges and other large rivers probably account for their ritual status in relation to other streams.

[1] Heinz-Gerhard Zimpel, "Vom Religionseinfluss in den Kulturlandschaften zwischen Taurus und Sinai," *Mitteilungen der Geographischen Gesellschaft in München*, XLVIII (1963), 136, is nevertheless justified in his opinion that the main task of ascertaining the effect of environment on religious forms devolves on the science of religion rather than on geography.

[2] "Religion, Landscape, and Space," *Landscape*, IX (Winter 1960), 14.

[3] The notion that "cleanliness is next to godliness" is an ancient one in Monsoon Asia.

Another well-known environmentalist proposition, now fairly discredited, has to do with the origins of monotheism. In the nineteenth century and early in this one, the desert, or sometimes more specifically the pastoral nomad life, was seen as the source of monotheist concepts. "Le désert est monothéiste" was the dictum of Ernest Renan, the nineteenth century French historian.[4] Combine the sight of the star-studded firmament, the harshness of desert existence, and a feeling of human insignificance, and monotheism must result, it was thought. Pastoral nomad society is dominantly patriarchal. A male leader is given the responsibility of coordinating the necessarily rapid responses of a highly mobile group confronted with day-to-day exigencies. A paternal god with a keen interest in the affairs of the tribe is, then, the way monotheism would surely be expressed, as a projection of the normal arrangements of pastoral life.

Apart from those that belong to the historical universalizing religions, some pastoral nomad groups seem to have a concept of a supreme Sky God. He is sometimes a do-nothing deity, not actively worshipped, and is usually associated with numerous minor deities, female as well as male. This concept is not confined to pastoralists; many of the simple ethnic religions of primitive hunting and gathering societies contain a belief in a high god, often regarded as the creator and preserver of the world. These simple religions are found in deserts, tropical forests, grasslands, temperate woodlands, and tundra.[5]

Monotheist concepts in the pre-Christian period were neither common to all pastoral nomads—the pre-Islamic Arabs had sun and moon divinities—nor were they exclusively confined to pastoral nomads or their sedentary descendants. Tentative statements of the monotheistic idea, understood as the worship of a single god-object, occur elsewhere, together with an abortive development of institutions and systems based on it. It appeared in the religion established by the Pharaoh Ikhnaton in the second millennium B.C., in the Zoroastrianism of Persia in the sixth century B.C., in Greek Stoicism, and even in the religion of the fifteenth century Texcocan ruler, Netzahualcoyotl. It is striking that all these developments took place among small groups of intelligentsia living in or near the cultural and administrative capitals of flourishing civilizations. Potentially universalizing, they appear as attempts to establish order in diversity consonant with the economic and political organization of their milieu. It does not seem likely that monotheist concepts held by migratory desert folk would have provided the key for these intellectual developments.

In the case of the strange, brief interlude of Egyptian Aton worship (a single god in the character of the sun), the proximity of the oasis civilization of the Nile Valley to the circulation routes of petty nomads of the Syrian steppe in fact points to diffusion in the other direction, that is, from high civilization to marginal steppe folk. This is what we should expect, since at the time the pastoralists of the lands bordering the great riverine civilizations were themselves marginal culture groups, with the

---

[4] Quoted by Pierre Deffontaines, *Géographie et religions* (Paris: Gallimard, 1948), p. 130 n.

[5] Opposing interpretations from the point of view of religious history are presented by W. A. Lessa and E. Q. Vogt, *Reader in Comparative Religion: an Anthropological Approach* (New York: Harper & Row, Publishers, Inc., 1958), pp. 24-46.

heavy flow of cultural items moving to them rather than in the opposite direction. As for the apparently monotheistic Hebrews and their sojourn in Egypt, the most reliable dating of any such event according to current Biblical scholarship would place it shortly after the Ikhnaton episode. Some scholars therefore wonder whether the sojourn of the Hebrews in Egypt might not have been responsible for the development among them of an ethical monotheism.

Ethical monotheism may have arisen from a need to bring rational order to a world of many cultures and classes. If so, it would illustrate the relation between the scope of a religion and the dimensions of the society conceiving it. Pastoral tribes, such as the Hebrews, and small commercially-oriented states, such as Israel and Judah, might well have a concept of a universal father and aspirations toward universal brotherhood.[6] A simple universalist ideology of this kind is by no means unique. Many simple tribal religions have some concept of universal human associations and universal moral obligations, although the concept of mankind may be limited by narrow geographical horizons. For example, the people of Burundi believe that "Kazikamuntu (which may mean Root-of-men) is the common ancestor of all mankind. . . . He had, among other children, Gatutsi, Gahutu, and Gatwa," these being the ancestors of the three major tribes of Burundi, the Tutsi, Hutu, and Twa. "Gatwa killed one of his brothers and for that reason was cursed by his father." [7]

Characteristically in ethnic religions, the supernatural agency involved in the creation of mankind stands in some special relationship to the tribe or nation. The relationship may be expressed through a special act of creation, a special revelation, or a special favor. This relationship is not shared by others and cannot be unless they are absorbed into the ethnos, or total cultural tradition, of the favored group.

The geographical condition that challenges this parochial position and permits the development of a truly universalizing religion is that of a political or commercial empire. There must be vigorous cultural flows along many routes, with cultural interchange occurring at many nodes; at the major nodes one should find, as a result, plural ethnic communities of merchants, artisans, literati, soldiers, and a proletariat. This situation is not alone sufficient for the successful sweep of a universalizing religion.[8] In certain circumstances, other arrangements may appear, such as the *millet* system of the Ottoman Empire (see Chapter 5).

It was the political and economic organization of the Roman Empire that made possible the universalizing of monotheism through the medium of Christianity. The early Christian message was addressed to the Jews as a national group at a time when a sense of involvement with the great nations of the world was growing among them. Nevertheless, among

[6] A current scholarly position suggests that the refinement and elaboration of this concept in Hebrew prophetic literature could have owed something to contemporary universalistic trends in Persia.

[7] J. J. Macquet, "The Kingdom of Ruanda," in *African Worlds: Studies in the Cosmological Ideas and Social Values of African Peoples*, ed. C. Daryll Forde (London: Published for the International African Institute by the Oxford University Press, 1954), p. 173.

[8] Toynbee, *A Study of History*, Vol. 4, p. 422, argues, but not without opposition, that universalizing religions appear at moments of imminent breakdown in the history of civilization. The machinery of a civilization is, in any case, understood to be prerequisite for the propagation of universalizing polyethnic religions.

the Jews in their homeland, the teaching and subsequent cult of Jesus seem to have created no more than a coterie of followers. Abroad, in cities with mixed immigrant populations, Jewish communities were more readily moved to support the new faith.

Two aspects of these "overseas" Jewish communities should be noted. Before the Roman destruction of the temple in Jerusalem, to be away from the land of Israel was to be partly de-Judaized. Jews abroad were exposed to much more vigorous alien cultural contacts than Jews in the home country and thus were more vulnerable to cultural change. Overseas Judaism had also accepted considerable numbers of non-Jews through contact conversion, especially in the seaport of Alexandria. These new Jews would be particularly receptive to a universalizing religion having Jewish antecedents.

The potential for ideological diffusion in this situation was realized when Paul gave Christianity its universalizing form by making it unnecessary for Christians to observe traditional Jewish law. Implanted in the homeland and among minority nuclei in the overseas Jewish communities, Christianity spread to other ethnic elements in the cities situated on the trade routes, including Rome. The cosmopolitan urban populations were, like the Jews among them, de-ethnicized, but they were not enthusiastic about the official Roman religion. Eastern religions were diffused in many provinces of the empire. Christianity, adopting the common social form of the mystery religions, was an attractive alternative, particularly among the underprivileged. The minority of the population to which it appealed at first was widely distributed in urban nuclei throughout the empire. It was Roman organization, a splendid network of roads linking together many commercial and garrison towns, that made this distribution possible.[9] Emporia such as Antioch and Alexandria, situated at the head of major routes penetrating into extra-Mediterranean environments, opened additional avenues for Christian expansion. In the second century, Irenaeus, one of the fathers of the Church, frankly acknowledged the importance of the Pax Romana to the propagation of Christianity and the organization of the Christian community. "Thanks to the Romans," he writes, "we can travel without fear on all the highways, and ships carry us wherever we wish to go."[10] Christian circulation was greatly increased late in the fourth century when Christianity was adopted as the official religion in the Roman territories: the network of empire became the network of the empire's church.

Ecology and Religious Institutions

In the simple ethnic systems, religion often seems to be almost entirely a ritualization of ecology. Religion is the medium whereby nature and natural processes are placated, cajoled, entreated, or manipulated in order to secure the best results for man. Even at a very primitive technological level, however, every culture operates selectively in taking its sa-

[9] By the end of the third century, there were many Christians in the army, especially in the western provinces, according to Toynbee, *A Study of History*, Vol. 7, pp. 340-41.
[10] Quoted by Gastone Imbrighi, *Lineamenti di geografia religiosa* (Rome: Editrice Studium, 1961), p. 73.

cred "resources" from its ecological milieu. The religious behavior of such societies becomes an extended commentary on selected, usually dominant, features of their economies. From this general condition among simple societies, something of the ritual and religion of late Paleolithic Europe has been inferred. A well-known cave painting in southern France is thus interpreted as a representation of a ritual dance associated with the hunt.[11]

Most sedentary or semisedentary agricultural folk in humid tropical lands and elsewhere have a great elaboration of ritual that is predominantly concerned with the natural cycle, the relationship between man and the land. Many tribal groups in insular Southeast Asia, both shifting (swidden) cultivators and sedentary wet-rice farmers sanctify each stage in the agricultural cycle by establishing a village quarantine, allowing no one in or out, and observing a taboo on all but special activities. These sacred moments in the agricultural calendar are known by various names —as *punen* among the Mentawei Island people to the west of Sumatra, as *pantang* among the Kayan and Kenyah of Sarawak, and as *obaya* among the Bontoc, the wet-rice cultivators of northern Luzon. The Bontoc have animal sacrifices and obaya periods, usually lasting for three days, on the following occasions: initial harrowing of paddy fields; preparation of seedbeds and sowing of seed; feast for growth of seedlings; feast of seven days preceding ceremonial planting of seedlings; completion of transplanting; sacrifice for vigorous growth of rice; preparation for harvest, initial harvest; and completion of harvest—a seven-day feast.[12]

Often, the requirements of agriculture are dramatically expressed in a variety of symbolic rituals, such as those of the Hopi, the skillful maize farmers of northeastern Arizona. "Shrines with prayer feathers are set up in the fields and skillful husbandry must be supported by individual and collective rites . . . ceremonial activities throughout the year have nearly always some reference to agricultural prosperity, while corn is used symbolically at every turn." [13] Hopi rites of ecological significance are the forced planting of corn and beans in the ritual underground chamber during the late winter; the planting of sticks carrying packets of corn seed when the land is being prepared; the running of foot races when the corn is planted to encourage swift growth; the rainmaking ceremonies, including the celebrated Snake Dance, toward the end of the season. The full annual cycle of religious ceremonies is much more than a ritualization of agriculture, however, for it also symbolizes the Hopi story of creation,[14] just as the ritualized agricultural calendar of the Hebrews was used to symbolize the major episodes in Jewish sacred history.

The selective character of this ritualization of ecology should again be stressed. Malinowski, for example, sees ritual as focussing on the unpredictable. Among the Melanesian Trobrianders an extensive magic

11 See Karl J. Narr, "Approaches to the Religion of Early Paleolithic Man," *History of Religions,* IV (1964), 18. The painting shows a masked man-like figure poised in the attitude of the dance and wearing or endowed with antlers, an animal skin, and a tail.
12 Alfredo G. Pacyaya, "Acculturation and Culture Change in Sagada," *Silliman Journal,* XI (March-June 1964), 24.
13 C. Daryll Forde, *Habitat, Economy, and Society: a Geographical Introduction to Ethnology* (London: Methuen & Company, Ltd., 1934), pp. 243, 245.
14 On this point, as well as for a superb description of the cycle of Hopi ceremonies, see Frank Waters, *Book of the Hopi* (New York: The Viking Press, 1963), Part III, "The Mystery Plays," pp. 125-250.

ritual is associated with deep-sea fishing, which is uncertain and dangerous, but few rites mark the productive but perfectly safe lagoon fishing.[15]

At times, myths and rituals crystallize around elements in a group's ecology that are archaic. A hunting people who have become agriculturalists may retain for a long time a great emphasis on ritual concerned with hunting rather than planting. A subsistence agricultural community that is drawn into a commercial exchange economy may continue the ritualization of its food plants without integrating important new cash crops in its ritual system.

Both the selectivity of cultures in sanctifying their economies through ritual and the occasional persistence of archaic ecologies in ritual form are illustrated at a more complex ecological level by the broad regional contrast between the primary ritual foods of the eastern Mediterranean and those of northern India. In Judaism, despite the pastoral milieu of its origins, it is bread and not milk that has ritual primacy. This particular selective assignment of sacred properties is perhaps common to other Mediterranean religious systems; it is retained in the essential symbolism of the Eucharist. In northern India, on the other hand, despite a predominantly agrarian economy based on the cultivation of field crops, it is the ancient pastoral staple, milk or its processed form *ghi*, that is the primary ritualized food among Hindus.

As society and economy become more complex, symbolization and abstraction of ecological matter increase, the process becoming intensified in the transition from ethnic to universalizing systems.[16] To illustrate this process, an extended comparison will be made of the way in which the annual biological cycle is treated in the religious calendars of Judaism, Christianity, and Islam.

In the religion of Deuteronomy and the later books of the Old Testament, little expression of the earlier pastoral ecology survives. There is a certain amount of sentimental attachment to the mores of the earlier period and some idealizing of them; but pastoralist patterns of self-government have been allowed to give way to the more impersonal and less easily checked bureaucracy, both secular and religious, of a petty agricultural-commercial state. The shepherd has moved from the center of the economic stage to a backward and impoverished sector on its margins, although he still constitutes a folk ideal, occasionally exercising moral force.[17] The pastoral origins of the new Israelite ethnos are used selectively to reinforce identity: the sacred groves of other peasant societies are abominated, as is the pig, associated with pagan fertility rites and despised by pastoralists; it marks the people who are slaves to the soil.

By the first millennium B.C., a religion of pastoral tribes has been incorporated in the religious system of an urbanized state with a temple, hereditary priesthood, fixed holy places in the Judaean hills, and national pilgrimages. Its religious calendar is now tied to the Mediterranean ecology of dry farming of winter grains (wheat and barley), tree cultivation, and a partial transhumance associated with the raising of sheep and goats.

[15] Bronislaw Malinowski, *Magic, Science, and Religion* (New York: The Free Press of Glencoe, Inc., 1948), pp. 12-13.

[16] In devising a new universalizing religion, for example, Zoroaster (Zarathustra) deliberately rejected most of the ecological material in the existing Persian ethnic religions; McNeill, *Rise of the West*, pp. 155-56.

[17] Cf. the embodiment of American virtues in the frontiersman and the cowboy.

Now, the Mediterranean environment and its associated agricultural seasons are sharply limited in extent, occupying about a hundredth of the earth's land surface.[18] The distinctive features of the Mediterranean ecology are the mild rainy winter and the very pronounced summer drought. Almost everywhere in the middle latitudes and much of the tropics, summer is the chief, if not the only, agricultural season, but this regime is reversed in Mediterranean lands, except where the advanced technology of irrigation can be used.

Fall, in the older agricultural pattern of Mediterranean lands, is no season of thanksgiving for the bounty of the summer just past, but the time for a somewhat austere rededication in preparation for the new agricultural year. There is also some apprehension as one waits at the appointed time for the early rains of October and November, so critical for agricultural success. But the austerity is not absolute. The stores of grain are not yet exhausted and some plants ingeniously adapted to the rigorous climatic regime produce food resources at this late season. These are the summer-ripening cucurbits and the xerophytic woody things domesticated in the area for their edible fruits, such as the pomegranate, the fig, and, above all, the grapevine. These ecological circumstances are reflected in the mood and attitude of the autumnal holy days of historic Jewish practice: Rosh Hashanah, the *New* Year; Yom Kippur,[19] the day of atonement in preparation for a new beginning; Succoth, the Feast of Booths, with its late offerings of fruit, an echo, too, perhaps, of the terminal summer encampment of pastoral folk.

Spring is quite another matter, combining in the Mediterranean the exultation of both rebirth and harvest. As happens elsewhere—in India during the monsoon rains, for example—the season when stocks grow thin just before the harvest is one symbolized by abstinence. A fast before the feast, perhaps a precautionary taboo, is found in the Jewish calendar, but the Christian observance of a long Lent does not make its appearance until the fourth century A.D. The ecological characteristics of the Mediterranean spring are reflected in the Jewish Passover and the Christian Easter. The seasonal connotation of Easter in the Mediterranean is rather different from its connotation in northern Europe. In both lands, it is biological renewal manifested in the blossoming of fruit trees and the ungainly sprightliness of new-born lambs and calves. But in the Mediterranean, spring is also the rewarding, if all has gone well, of labor and the proper religious observances. In April, the discomforts of winter are over, the fields are full of ripening grain from the late fall sowing, and the hillsides are verdant with a new cover of annual grasses on which flocks and herds can fatten. For pastoralist and farmer alike, it is the season of plenty. This, then, was the season of joyous thanksgiving and full-hearted reaffirmation, a truly popular holiday. The ethnic religious institutions called for both private spring-cleaning of a ritual kind and public observances, involving offerings of the first of the produce of field and flock.

---

[18] The quantitative definition of the *Cs* climate type in the internationally used Köppen system of climate classification is taken as a suitable approximation.

[19] This holy day is thought to be a late, post-Exilic addition to the Jewish calendar, but it has its origins in the sacred period following the autumn new moon feast of the New Year.

The Passover season was not the end of the Mediterranean agricultural cycle. "Seven times seven days shall you tally: when the sickle is first put to the standing grain, you shall begin a tally of seven weeks." [20] Seven weeks from the first reaping of barley to the completion of the wheat harvest and one comes to the last great seasonal holy day of the Old Testament calendar before the long dry summer sets in—Shabuoth, the Feast of Weeks.

These sacred agricultural festivals were given additional symbolic meanings from sacred history and both kinds of sacred significance were retained in the Judaism of the Diaspora. This is what makes Judaism an ethnic religion. Based on the Old Testament material, the major Jewish holidays are still celebrated verbally and to some extent symbolically as if taking place on the eastern shore of the Mediterranean three thousand years ago. The harvest first fruits are symbolically offered in April, wherever one may be, and the seven-week tally is recorded, however distant in place and time from fields of standing grain. Only in a secular *sotto voce* in certain domestic rites are the contemporary circumstances conceded to be no longer those conjured up in the liturgy.

Christianity has retained only a few elements of this sacred Mediterranean calendar. By discarding much of it, freeing itself from the bonds of place, Christianity could become more successfully universalizing. The Christian significance of Easter retains the seasonally appropriate motifs of sacrificial offering and rebirth, forcefully combined in the concept of resurrection. The symbolism of the sacrifice of the Passover (Paschal) lamb is a particularly important element here. In Latin and the Romance languages, the Christian sacred festival has a name similar to the Hebrew word for Passover. It is different in the north, where Christianity did not take hold until some time after it had become the Roman state religion. The customs celebrating the arrival of spring after the long, cold northern winter had clustered around the goddess of the season, Eastre or Ostara. Since her festival coincided with the Christian sacred season, her name was retained, while some of the symbolism of the pagan season survived in folk customs.

For another part of the Christian sacred calendar, one of the popular and widespread pagan cults of the Roman world was drawn on, while the remaining Jewish festivals were subordinated or eliminated. On the basis of circumstantial evidence, scholars are now inclined to place the season of Christ's birth in late summer or early fall, around the time of the Jewish New Year. But the event was not celebrated in the early Church, and was only later fixed to coincide with the date of the birth of the sun god, Sol Invictus, associated with the winter solstice. In northern Europe, both the popular name of the Christmas season, Yule, and the folk customs that surround it are frank retentions of pagan religious celebrations of the winter solstice.

The Christian calendar, because of its exotic origin, contains a sacral gap for non-Mediterranean Europe. It lacks a special celebration of the harvest season. Hints of the pagan celebrations once performed at this season barely survive in northern European folk customs associated with Michaelmas (September 29) and All Hallows' Eve or Hallowe'en (Octo-

[20] Deuteronomy 16:9.

ber 31). The success of Thanksgiving Day, a semireligious occasion which partly copies a feature of an Eastern Woodland Indian religion, and its firm place in the American national iconography point to an ecological inadequacy in the Christian calendar when it is used outside the Mediterranean hearth.

The Christian calendar becomes even less appropriate ecologically in mid-latitude countries in the Southern Hemisphere, where Easter occurs in the fall and Christmas comes in early summer. The symbolic seasonal connotations are thereby lost. Other symbolic malfunctions of this sort appear in Christianity. The potent symbolism of lamb and shepherd (Christ is called "The Good Shepherd"), rich in meaning for Mediterranean peoples, cannot be conveyed literally to many tropical agriculturalists. Missionaries carrying the message of Christianity to such people have had to contrive other symbols to replace these traditional ones.

The Islamic calendar has, by contrast with the Christian, detached itself far more completely from ecological bonds. As in the Jewish, Hindu, and Buddhist calendars, the basic unit of the Islamic calendar is the lunar month, twelve of which comprise a year of 354 days. To maintain some correspondence between the sequence of lunar months and the annual climatic and biological cycles which are related to the solar year of 365¼ days, most lunar calendars make one of a variety of adjustments, such as the adding of a thirteenth lunar month in certain years. The Muslim calendar, following Muhammad's express instruction in the Koran, does not do this. A Muslim month such as Ramadan, the period of daytime fasting, will slide through the seasons of cold and heat, rain and drought, without relevance for these conditions. It is proper to complete the pilgrimage to Mecca in the Islamic month called Dhu'l-hijja, "The Month of Pilgrimage," whether this falls in summer or winter, an alternation that occurs within a span of two decades. Because of this, in some years more than others, observance of the Islamic calendar disrupts the annual economic cycle of agricultural folk like the fellahin of Egypt or the rice farmers of East Pakistan.

The Islamic calendar is thus liberated from ecological ties. It becomes a program of ritual and devotional experiences which can be followed in any kind of climatic environment without incongruity and with equal appropriateness north or south of the equator. How did this come about? Perhaps because Islam was from the beginning a religion of the town. Mecca and Medina, the towns that cradled Islam, depended on long-distance trade rather than on central services to agricultural hinterlands. Caravan and sea trade had a seasonal rhythm, but the regulatory storage mechanisms in towns and the flexible work patterns of merchants and artisans would dilute the significance of the seasons, not very pronounced in that low-latitude desert situation. The significance of the seasons for townspeople would be further weakened by the psychological and social distance separating them from oasis cultivators, as is apparent in early Islamic attitudes (Chapter 3). The fellahin have to cultivate by a calendar related to the solar year, and this calls for special local almanacs relating agricultural events to the Muslim calendar in any given year. Separate farmers' calendars are maintained in Yemen and Hadhramaut, where the system of time-reckoning by the stars goes back to the pre-Islamic period. The Hindu lunar calendar in Bengal and Christian solar calendars in Turkey, Syria, and Egypt are used by Muslims there concurrently with the Muslim religious calendar.

The often archaic quality of the traits ritualized by tribal societies has already been noted. A similar archaism is evident today in the slow adjustment of universalizing systems, including Christianity, to the vastly changed ecological conditions of a highly industrialized society. Judaism and Christianity maintain the rhythm of a pre-industrial society and the tempo of the modern western world has made this rhythm obsolete. What significance can a Sabbath day of rest have for a society that is ready to embrace the four-day work week? And what are the special occasions in this society that call for sanctification? They are to be found in the calendars of the modern quasi religions, nationalism and Communism, in the various Memorial Days, Labor Days, and May Days that celebrate nationalist martyrdoms and the yields of industrial organization.

CHAPTER 3 *religion and the land*

One concern of the geography of religions is how the land provides a record of religious systems, their associated institutions, and the patterns of religiously conditioned behavior. A fairly full inventory has been made of the more conspicuous landscape features associated with historic and contemporary religious systems, but there have been few attempts to assess the intensity of religion's impress on the land. Some examples of the religious transformation of landscape will be discussed here, focusing on the differences among religious systems.

Formal Positive Expression of Religion on Landscape

The form, orientation, and density of sacred structures, use of the land in cemeteries, and special assemblages of plants and animals for religious purposes are among effects on the land of the formally prescriptive, traditional aspects of religious systems. While the list of items considered here is incomplete, it points to work already done and current lines of inquiry.

SACRED STRUCTURES. Among simple ethnic religions where ecological relationships are direct and intense, sacred structures are neither widely nor conspicuously distributed. Certain objects and structures may be revered, but they are usually not extraordinary. A pile dwelling, perhaps more ornate than others, may be the skullhouse of Indonesian cultivators who invest head-hunting with religious meaning. The cult objects of nomadic peoples must be portable, like the ancient Hebrew ark of the covenant, or designed for temporary use, like the altar of earth erected in a number of designated sacred locations.[1]

---

[1] Exodus 20:24.

There are evident ecological limitations to man's conception of the sacred and to the ways in which he marks the world around him as sacred. Yet at similar technological levels, striking variations occur in the form and prominence of sacred structures. Much more imposing structures than the Indonesian cult house occur in simple, pre-literate societies having a comparable technology. However, such structures occur only with some stratification of society and with a specialized priesthood, as in eastern Polynesia, where priests and distinct social classes were found. The sacred village places there contained immense stone terraces enclosed by standing monoliths.

The presence of monumental sacred structures raises questions about the ecology and spatial organization of the societies involved. How productive must a group be to allocate labor and technical skills to such works? How large must it be? Is a stratified social order a requisite for the organization of effort? Archeology provides a number of puzzling cases of disproportionately grand religious structures associated with a simple technological base. Examples are the megalithic tombs, avenues, and circles of Atlantic Europe in the second millennium B.C. and the great pyramidal mounds of the prehistoric Mississippi Valley cultures. These point to the emergence of a religious system able to harness labor from a wide area without employing the political mechanisms characteristic of the city and state. A diffusion of technology and ideological motivation from external centers of civilization has been suggested. The western Mediterranean and Atlantic megalithic culture, represented by the great stone circles of Avebury and Stonehenge, is interpreted as a spreading of skills, organization, and religious ideas, ultimately from an eastern Mediterranean hearth.[2]

The use of large amounts of labor for construction of stone monuments is ecologically more appropriate when the structures are ritual foci in well-populated, productive regions, as in early dynastic Egypt and in the Valley of Mexico long before the historic Aztec civilization. The organization necessary for the construction of pyramids suggests that the religious systems were of a compound ethnic type, but we do not know whether these ritual complexes in fact had other urban functions. The Mayan temple-cities, later buried in the Guatemalan jungle, seem not to have functioned as urban nuclei, but only as ritual foci.

The construction, maintenance, and continued use of such large cult assemblages may well create an ecological imbalance. We do not really know what demands on labor and resources a simple society can support without danger, especially in the humid tropics. In Cambodia and Ceylon, a severe strain apparently was placed on the economy by the temple-building programs of Buddhist kings, leading to the displacement of advanced civilizations. The perimeter wall of the temple complex at Angkor Wat in Cambodia is 7½ miles long; the work must have required tens of thousands of people supported by a highly productive agriculture, but little remains of this.[3]

[2] McNeill, *Rise of the West*, pp. 98-102, "Megalithic Protocivilization." McNeill speaks of "missionaries" of a megalithic religion which may have "promised some form of life after death" (p. 100).

[3] W. Credner, "Kultbauten in der hinterindischen Landschaft," *Erdkunde*, XII (1947), 48-61.

Imbalances are perhaps more likely to occur when a foreign religious system, like Buddhism in Southeast Asia, organizes an area of simple economy. Roman Catholic churches in technologically retarded areas are often substantial structures, surpassing in size and splendor anything else in the indigenous landscape. Spanish governors in sixteenth century Mexico deplored the excessive building of churches, complaining that it withdrew large amounts of Indian labor from the productive economy.

A striking aspect of megalith and temple construction is the great effort often expended to obtain stone. Blocks of bluestone were transported from southern Wales to Salisbury Plain for some of the Stonehenge monoliths. The motive was probably religious, the permanence of stone making it particularly appropriate for certain sacred structures.[4]

Complex ethnic and universalizing religious systems usually impress a widely diffused pattern of sacred structures on the landscape. A standard religious structure may occur profusely over wide areas. Such communal sacred buildings differ in form, space requirements, and density according to the ideological and organizational needs of the religious system.

The important variable in the size and density of the repeated, modular religious structure—church, mosque, temple—is its primary religious function. A broad distinction can be made between the structure which houses a congregation and one which houses a god.

Neither function has much place in some religious systems. In the Chinese religion and the Roman religion of the early Republic, the most important rites were performed in the home. The Chinese temple, housing the village or clan god or the specialized "departmental" gods having regional or national importance, is secular in appearance. Such gods need only a modest amount of ritual attention, while their temples may actually serve more important functions: a clan "temple" is the business meeting place of the living representatives of the clan as well as an ancestral memorial. Other temples were maintained by the government, and rites for the welfare of the state were performed there by the resident official. These temples looked like administrative buildings; their size corresponded to the administrative rank of the town where they were located.

Hinduism, too, has its household gods; the ancient Vedic religion of the Indo-European invaders had no other form of worship. Hinduism also has its inconspicuous village shrines. Its remaining gods are many, however, and are generally well housed in temples supported by caste groups or by wealthy individuals. The total wealth of Hindu temples is impressive; they are said to own $1,000,000,000 worth of jewelry and property. Each temple houses one or more gods, whose clientele may overlap those of many other temples. These do not constitute congregations, nor is there a territorial hierarchy, although the temples are operated by hereditary ritualists. Size and density of temples are related to local productivity and local decisions concerning allocation of resources, although drafts on regional resources for the construction and maintenance of impressive temples used to be made by feudal rulers.

---

[4] This megalithic symbolism survives in the Christian metaphor of the rock on which the Church was founded, while the sacred focus of Islam is the megalith of the Kaaba in Mecca, whose cult Muhammad was obliged for political reasons to absorb into his own puritanically monotheistic religion.

As the house of a god, the Hindu temple has architectural and spatial features which distinguish it from church or mosque. It does not need a large, closed, interior space. The god—in the form of a stone or wooden artifact—is often concealed in a dimly lit inner shrine. Farther out there is space for ritual processions and for public circulation. There are pavilions and pillared corridors and, in South India, elaborate temple gateways. The grounds, usually walled as sacred space, must house the Brahman caretakers of the resident deity together with the artisans and other specialists who serve the temple, and the layout must include a large pool for the ritual baths of both gods and men.

Houses of gods in other religions usually display the essential features of the Hindu temple. Ancient Greek temples provided no interior space for the public, who could only watch ceremonies held in the open. The holy of holies is often darkened, as in Solomon's temple,[5] in keeping with its mystery.

Religions which must house a congregation have different arrangements of space. Judaism has the synagogue or *beth ha-keneseth*, "the house of the assembly (or congregation)." The Muslim building usually called a mosque in English is properly the *jāmi'*, from the word for "assembly"; most small structures, often a room or annex, are known simply as *masjid* (whence "mosque"), "a place of worship."

The function, and hence the structure, of the Christian church is ambivalent, and historically a tension has existed between its two possible functions. In early Christianity, the church was considered a house of congregation. With the emergence of Christianity as an approved religion, the concept was elaborated on the model of the *basilica*, the Roman place of civil assembly. In the Roman, Eastern Orthodox, and Oriental churches, however, the evolution of the priestly management of ritual led to the development of the altar as the focus of ritual mystery. This trend was reversed in northern Europe after the Reformation, especially among the nonconformist or free churches, while the Puritans and Quakers went very far in modifying the function of the church as the special home of a divine presence. The two functions are reflected in different names in European languages. "Church" and the related Germanic forms (e.g., kirk, *Kirche*) are from the Greek *kyriakon doma*, "the house of the Lord," while French *église*, Spanish *iglesia*, and related Romance words are derived from the Greek *ekklesia*, meaning an "assembly." Curiously, the primary function and the etymological meaning seem to be reversed in the two linguistic regions. Even in the Protestant systems, however, an architecturally and spatially distinct structure for religious activity is a firmly embedded tradition, so that the smallest community tries to have one.

Thus Christianity differs from Judaism and Islam in its landscape impress. In Islam, space for community worship is the main architectural consideration. In cities with large congregations, the architectural techniques of the Byzantine Empire were elaborated to provide soaring enclosed spaces completely devoid of plastic representations of sanctity. But the great mosques are exceptional, confined to the larger cities. There is no Islamic equivalent of the European parish church, especially

[5] I Kings 8:12.

not the rural church, nor anything like a Protestant community church. In many Islamic countries, the rural place of prayer is undistinguished —mud houses, thatched huts, and, in an ancient Muslim tradition, demarcated open spaces serve the purpose, even in densely populated lands like Egypt and Bengal. In the Muslim parts of Negro Africa and in Southeast Asia, the ensemble of dome and minaret became common only in the last century.

Islam and Judaism evidently have less need than Christianity does for a sanctified house. In these religions, only the community can provide the proper context of worship, and it is this which invests synagogue and mosque with their sanctity. A Jewish religious service is fundamentally incomplete unless a minimum "community" of ten adult males is present; whether or not the service is held in a synagogue is actually of little importance.

In Islam, there is a marked contrast between the frequency of town mosques and country mosques. This goes back to the relationship between Islam and the Islamic ruler, the administrative head of the religious community. In early Islam, the building of a mosque was the obligation of the ruler, and the Friday service, obligatory for all male Muslims, had to be conducted by him. This reinforced the strong predilection for the city which runs through Islam. The Hanafi school of Islamic law, which prevails in the Arabic Muslim world except for northwest Africa, permits the Friday communal service to be held only in large towns, while the Shafi'i school further restricts this to allow the service in one mosque only in each town, if the single large mosque is able to hold the community. Von Grunebaum writes: "The legislation of the Koran envisages city life . . . Only in a city, that is, a settlement harboring a central mosque, jāmi', fit for the Friday service, and a market (and preferably a public bath) can all the requirements of the faith be properly fulfilled." [6]

From the thirteenth and fourteenth centuries, the building of small mosques and their endowment by local people of wealth became common and spread to the villages. These small mosques had a social function—providing a meeting place for villagers, a school house, or a resting place for travellers—as much as a religious one and were often inconspicuous. A count of 800 mosques in Cairo around 1000 A.D. and of 1,500 mosques in Damascus seems not to refer to free-standing buildings alone but must include large numbers of mosques that are no more than rooms in residential structures and bazaars.[7]

What can be said about the relative impress on the land made by the distribution of church, mosque, or temple in different religious systems? Estimates of density based on map analysis can be made, and ratios of population to communal sacred structure can be calculated. Variations in the size and form of the cult unit in different religious systems, and the different appropriations of energy that this implies, would complicate interpretation of the results. In American cities, for example, the Roman Catholic Church is often the most conspicuous religious structure,

    [6] Gustave E. von Grunebaum, *Medieval Islam* (Chicago: University of Chicago Press, 1946), pp. 173-74.
    [7] Zimpel, "Vom Religionseinfluss in den Kulturlandschaften zwischen Taurus und Sinai," *Mitteilungen der Geographischen Gesellschaft in München*, XLVIII (1963), 138.

occupying the largest tract of land. A certain congregation size is consciously aimed at in the spacing of Catholic churches and the Catholic system places greater value on the grandeur of the church edifice than does the typical Protestant ideology.[8]

Major religious systems seem to produce rather regularly a unit structure for every few hundred adherents. A deviation toward low figures is noticeable among the minor Protestant denominations, in which churches may serve religious communities of less than 100 persons. Deviations in the other direction may have several causes: the system may be expanding rapidly; there may be a low level of adherence; or the religious system may have a program which deliberately provides only one structure to several thousand persons.

A large Deccan village has a ratio of one temple to 440 Hindus [9] while a small Gujerati town has a ratio nearer one to 500.[10] Many of these are lower-caste temples and may not be separate or distinct structures. Larger temples are built by the larger and wealthier castes, and their distribution varies accordingly. Thus one should expect Gujerat to have a more conspicuously "religious" impress than the North Bihar plain, although the latter has a higher population density, and casual observation seems to bear this out. A Chinese town of 40,000 had, in the 1930's, about 70 officially recognized clan and local cult temples, giving a ratio of 570 persons per unit.[11]

Churches in the Muslim Middle East are very numerous in areas where Christianity is locally dominant; in the Maronite Christian area of Lebanon, there is said to be almost one per farmstead.[12] In Czarist Russia, on the other hand, as few as one village in ten might have a church, those having one (*selo*) being administratively distinguished from the others (*derevnya*).[13] A small town in central Italy had a ratio of one church for every 670 inhabitants in 1950, whereas the ratio had been about one church to 225 persons as recently as the early 1600's.[14]

In Cincinnati, Ohio, in the 1940's, the ratio of all church units to population, adhering or not, was just about one per thousand. The ratio for Catholic churches was one to 2,500, compared to an approximate national average of one church for every 2,000 Catholics. However, for the church-going Catholic population, the ratio was only one to 1,300. For the much smaller Jewish population of Cincinnati, the ratio was one institution (synagogue or Reformed temple) to 1,150 members, whereas the national data suggest that the average size of a Jewish congregation, whether practicing or not, is about 3,000. On the basis of membership figures, all "regular" Protestant denominations in Cincinnati which reported mem-

[8] Wesley A. Hotchkiss, *Areal Pattern of Religious Institutions in Cincinnati*. Department of Geography Research Paper No. 13, University of Chicago (Chicago, 1950), pp. 84, 94.

[9] O. H. K. Spate, *India and Pakistan: a General and Regional Geography* (London: Methuen & Company, Ltd., 1954), pp. 173-76.

[10] V. A. Janaki and Z. A. Sayed, *The Geography of Padra Town*. Maharaja Sayajirao University Geographical Series No. 1 (Baroda: Maharaja Sayajirao University of Baroda Press, 1962), pp. 32-41 and Map XXX.

[11] John K. Shryock, *The Temples of Anking and Their Cults: a Study of Modern Chinese Religion* (Paris, 1931).

[12] Zimpel, *op. cit.*, p. 138.

[13] Deffontaines, *Géographie et religions* (Paris: Gallimard, 1948), p. 128.

[14] Edward Price, "Viterbo: Landscape of an Italian City," *Annals*, Association of American Geographers, LIV (1964), 268 ff.

bership had an average per church of 330, ranging from 600 for the American Baptists, high compared to their national average, to 90 for the Church of the Nazarene.[15] The territorial organization of the Mormon Church sets a figure of 750 as the ideal population of a ward, the organizational equivalent of the parish; in 1949, the average ward size was 631.[16]

The landscapes that are most conspicuously impregnated with the marks of religious institutions may not be those of Monsoon Asia or the Muslim world, as is sometimes supposed. The impression of an abundance of religious objects in Asian landscapes may be a distorted European view provoked by the unfamiliar appearance of mosque and temple. One has only to visit those parts of Monsoon Asia which have a large Christian population, such as Goa, Cochin, and the west coast of Ceylon, to be struck by the assertiveness of Christianity in their landscapes. It is Christendom that seems to have made the most conspicuous impress of this kind. Its effect is perhaps most intense in the Catholic areas of northern Italy and southern Germany or in the rural American Midwest, with its multiplicity of Protestant denominations and sects, each having relatively small congregations but each firmly putting its mark on the land in the form of a distinctive church structure.

The visual religious impress is also conveyed by other structures. Wayside shrines and stone crosses occur profusely in Catholic lands like Bavaria and Austria, whereas Judaism and Protestantism do not have comparable symbolic structures. Islam, despite puritanist objections, uses the grave mosque or tomb to commemorate its saints in some countries, and probably, to judge from the hilltop location of many of them, to incorporate some pre-Muslim local sanctity. Bell-shaped shrines to departed holy men are a common feature in many Buddhist countries. The *chortens* of Tibet, the fields of *stupas* in the Central Burma plain, and the hundreds of ruined *dagabas* in the dry jungles of Ceylon are evidence of the way Buddhism in the past has been able to integrate territories lacking in political development.

LAND PATTERNS OF RELIGIOUS ORIGIN. Students of religious phenomena point out that most religious systems see a correspondence between the events and structure of the supernatural world and those of the human one. Religious man, Eliade suggests, goes further: his integration or "cosmicization" of unknown territories is "always a consecration; to organize space is to repeat the paradigmatic work of the gods." [17] The study of man's application of the cosmic or ideal pattern to the earth's surface

[15] Cincinnati data from Hotchkiss, *Religious Institutions in Cincinnati.* National data from Edwin S. Gaustad, *Historical Atlas of Religion in America* (New York: Harper & Row, Publishers, Inc., 1962) and H. Wakelin Coxill and Sir Kenneth Grubb, eds., *World Christian Handbook, 1962* (London: World Dominion Press, 1962).
[16] Thomas F. O'Dea, *The Mormons* (Chicago: University of Chicago Press, 1957), p. 180.
[17] Mircea Eliade, *The Sacred and the Profane: the Nature of Religion* (New York: Harper & Row, Publishers, Inc., 1961), p. 32; the idea is elaborated in his Chapter I: "Sacred Space and Making the World Sacred," pp. 20-67. On the same theme, see Erich Isaac, "The Act and the Covenant: the Impact of Religion on the Landscape," *Landscape,* XI (Winter 1962), 12-17, and "Religious Geography and the Geography of Religion," in *Man and the Earth,* University of Colorado Studies, Series in Earth Sciences, No. 3 (Boulder: University of Colorado Press, July 1965), pp. 1-14.

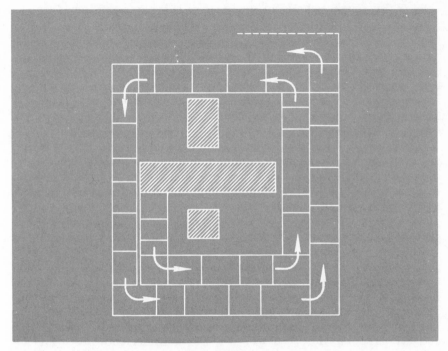

FIG. 1. *The Dogon cosmic field pattern: counterclockwise spiral extension of cultivated land around three original fields. (Redrawn from Griaule and Dieterlen, "The Dogon," in* African Worlds.)

is what Erich Isaac understands to be "religious geography." [18] Elsewhere, he distinguishes between a religious patterning of the land, which he thinks is associated with religions having a "cosmic ritual myth," and the amorphous impress of religion associated with those that do not.[19]

An example of the former is the remarkable cosmic design reflected in the field pattern of the Dogon swidden cultivators of Mali, near the Upper Volta border (Fig. 1).

The country of the Dogon has been organized as far as possible in accordance with the principle that the world developed in the form of a spiral. In theory, the central point of development is formed by three ritual fields, assigned to three of the mythical ancestors and to the three fundamental cults. When laid out, they mark out a world in miniature on which the gradual establishment of man takes place. Starting from these three fields, the fields belonging to the various kin groups, and finally various individual fields, are sited along the axis of a spiral starting from this central area.[20]

[18] "Religious Geography and the Geography of Religion," *Man and the Earth,* especially pp. 5-7.
[19] "The Act and the Covenant: the Impact of Religion on the Landscape," *Landscape,* XI (Winter 1962), 12-17.
[20] Marcel Griaule and Germaine Dieterlen, "The Dogon," in *African Worlds: Studies in the Cosmological Ideas and Social Values of African Peoples,* ed. C. Daryll Forde (London: Published for the International African Institute by the Oxford University Press, 1954), p. 94.

Eliade stresses the theme of the universe unfolding from some central point where man makes his home. "Just as the universe unfolds from a center and stretches out toward the cardinal points, the village . . . in Bali, as in some parts of Asia . . . comes into existence around an intersection." [21] The Balinese pattern may derive from India, where it appears here and there in the layout of field, village, and town. A pattern of axial north-south and east-west lines seems to be a secularized extension of the Hindu temple plan, itself "the earthly reproduction of a transcendent model." [22]

In antiquity and after the Renaissance, the grid town appears as a device characterizing a bureaucratic order, although not without ideological connotations. In its later use by certain religious communities, the grid plan may reflect an ideal cosmic plan. The Mormon use of a form of grid in their planned communal settlements, notable for their large square blocks, follows the plan for the City of Zion revealed in the Mormon sacred tradition (Fig. 2).

CEMETERIES. The allocations of space needed for the Jewish, Christian, and Muslim institution of burial in a community ground distinguish these religions from the Hindu, Buddhist, and Japanese, where the dead are cremated.[23] The Chinese, who bury their dead and commemorate them, are at variance with other Oriental religions. It has been suggested that a relationship exists between a sense of history and the custom of marked burial in civilized societies; Hindu-Buddhist cremation would fit civilizations with an ahistorical, "cyclical" world-view.

The contemporary "American way of death" has its counterpart in the traditional Chinese system, as well as such ancient societies as the Egyptian and Etruscan.[24] Societies such as these, with a concern for visible commemoration of the dead, may make pressing demands on space and other resources. In pre-Communist China, family graves placed on family agricultural land to fulfill religious requirements aggravated population pressure on the land. About 2 per cent of the arable land in the North China Plain, and as much as 10 per cent in some areas, was thus kept out of agricultural production. Similar pressures on cemetery land appear within crowded Western conurbations, although planners are often pleased to have these green "breathing spaces" left. They might be used as parks, as they are in Muslim countries like Iran, if the idea were not reprehensible to many Christians.

AGGREGATIONS AND DISPERSALS OF PLANTS AND ANIMALS. Many religions confer on certain plants and animals a measure of sanctity or special ritual function. The plants and animals which a religion prizes may be dispersed along the system's migration and circulation routes, and unnatural concentrations of these biotic forms may appear. The sacred In-

[21] Eliade, op. cit., p. 45.
[22] Ibid., p. 58.
[23] Numerous simple ethnic systems, especially of nomadic gathering, hunting, and pastoral folk, have little or no commemoration of the dead. The pre-Buddhist Mongols were a notable example, adjacent to the Chinese civilization with its diametrically opposite convention.
[24] Deffontaines, op. cit., pp. 43-67, 178-196, has much information on the "geography of the dead."

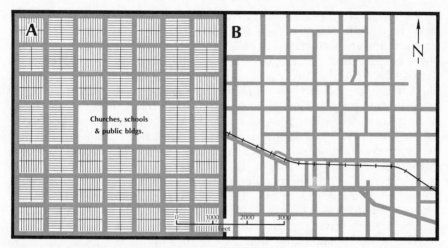

FIG. 2. *The Mormon City of Zion: the plan and its implementation.* A: *Joseph Smith's plan of "The City of Zion," 1833. (Adapted from Nelson,* The Mormon Village.) B: *American Fork, Utah,* ca. *1950.*

dian *pipal* or *bo* tree, which has no economic significance and little ornamental value, has been taken by the Buddhists from its North Indian habitat to distant Ceylon and Japan.[25] The dispersal of the cultivated citron in the Mediterranean in Roman times is attributed to Jewish ritual requirements,[26] while Muslim use of the Yemen white iris as a graveside flower is said to have dispersed that plant all over the Middle East.[27]

The sacral value of grape wine in Judaism and in most Christian systems led to cultivation of the vine beyond the Mediterranean. Christian monks made wine from it along the Rhine and Moselle, and less successfully as far north as the North and Baltic seas. One of the first innovations of nineteenth century Jewish settlers in Palestine was the reestablishment of grape cultivation in order to meet their ritual needs.

Cult preoccupation with certain plant and animal properties may have stimulated some domestication and selective breeding. White horses, long-horned African cattle, and turmeric, which yields a Hindu ritual pigment, are among the biotic forms thought to have been profoundly modified by man for ritual ends.[28] The relationship of ritual function to the selection and dispersal of many other domesticated plants and animals remains to be elucidated.

NAMES ON THE LAND. Place names (toponyms) having religious associations usually record a particular historic opportunity for a religious system to fix itself in place and time; some toponyms, however, may refer

[25] Paul Fickeler, "Fundamental Questions in the Geography of Religions," in *Readings in Cultural Geography,* ed. and trans. Philip L. Wagner and Marvin W. Mikesell (Chicago: The University of Chicago Press, 1962), p. 113.
[26] Erich Isaac, "The Influence of Religion on the Spread of Citrus," *Science,* CXXIX:3343 (January 23, 1959), 179-86.
[27] Zimpel, *op. cit.,* p. 143.
[28] H. Epstein, "Domestication Features in Animals as Functions of Human Society," in *Readings in Cultural Geography,* p. 293; David E. Sopher, "Indigenous Uses of Turmeric (*Curcuma domestica*) in Asia and Oceania," *Anthropos,* LIX (1964), 93-127.

to a prior local sanctity. The study of such place names has been chiefly concerned with places named for saints (hagiotoponyms) [29] which are common in predominantly Catholic lands. However, this "christening" of the landscape is not of the same order in the Old World as in the New. Where the Spanish, Portuguese, and French, directed by or conscious of the Church, settled in New World lands that had been sparsely occupied by primitive peoples, saints' names and other religious terms are likely to be numerous as place names. In time they appear as the names of large cities. Thus, five of California's seven largest cities have names with a religious connotation. The greatest density of hagiotoponyms, and the highest proportion of them to all kinds of place names, occurs where the New World Catholic population has been a conservative, dispersed, rural one of European origin. This condition is epitomized in French Quebec, where places take their names from the originally isolated parish churches, each serving a band of separate homesteads (Fig. 3A).

Where the Indian population and its net of place names was more dense, the cover of hagiotoponyms is less complete. Some Indian place names have been displaced or supplemented by Christianizing names, such as the doubly sacred San Juan Teotihuacan.[30] On the 1:5,000,000 map of Mexico, the pre-Spanish high culture area in the southern and central half, with at present more than four times the population density of the formerly more primitive northern half, has less than a third of all hagiotoponyms. The great majority of these southern names consist of saints' names added to pre-Spanish bases, an infrequent usage in northern Mexico.

In Europe, the land was Christianized over a long span of time and within a Roman or post-Roman urban framework. Saints' names began to appear as place names in Italy only in the late Middle Ages (ca. 1200-1400 A.D.),[31] and then predominantly as the names of offshoot hamlets, settlements growing around churches and abbeys, and isolated farmsteads (Fig. 3B). Much the same happened in France, saints' names becoming most frequent in the western zones of dispersed settlement. Deffontaines suggests that the frequency of hagiotoponyms in different French districts is directly related to the degree of population dispersal.[32]

Place-name study in non-Christian lands might provide useful information regarding the establishment of religious institutions there. In southern India, for example, the prefix *tiru-*, indicating sanctity, occurs in scattered place names, usually of peaks, inselbergs, and headlands, all commonly recognized as hierophanies, manifestations of the sacred. The distribution of such place names, including the thousands honoring different Hindu gods, should tell something about the direction and date of religious currents and the way in which local sanctity has been institutionalized in India.

---

[29] Gastone Imbrighi, *Lineamenti di geografia religiosa* (Rome: Editrice Studium, 1961), p. 163, uses the term *hierotoponomastics* for the study of the sacred as expressed in place names and refers to place names commemorating saints as *hagiotoponyms.*

[30] Teotihuacan, site of the great Toltec religious complex containing the Pyramid of the Sun, means "Place of the Gods" in Nahuatl, the language of the Aztecs.

[31] Imbrighi, *op. cit.*, p. 163.

[32] *Op. cit.*, p. 126.

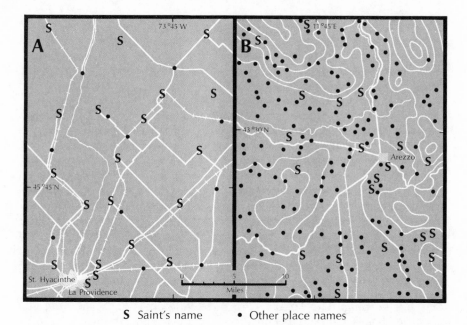

S Saint's name   • Other place names

FIG. 3. *Saints' names as place names.* A: *Quebec.* B: *Tuscany. All named places appearing on current 1:250,000 scale topographic maps are shown here.*

Formal Negative Expression of Religion on Landscape

Many of the prohibitions by which societies circumscribe behavior affect their environment directly, becoming conspicuous by the resultant absence of otherwise expectable conditions. Some religious prohibitions which directly affect the land—taboos on food, on work, and on certain economic activities—are considered here.

FOOD TABOOS.   Food taboos are of particular geographical interest since they differ from one religion to another,[33] sometimes producing sharp contrasts in agricultural economy within the same region. In pre-Muslim Persia, for example, the Manichaeans required a strict vegetarianism while the Zoroastrians encouraged eating meat as a way of acquiring supernatural power. Many food taboos are not formulated explicitly as part of a religious system, although certain religious concepts may underlie them.

Many simple religions have taboos on the killing and eating of certain animals, sometimes affecting the ecological balance. The Batak of Sumatra are said to have given up sedentary agriculture because tigers, protected by taboo, preyed on their buffaloes.[34] These taboos are mostly totemistic, but ethical and aesthetic attitudes also appear, as in taboos on the killing

[33] Frederick J. Simoons, *Eat Not This Flesh* (Madison: The University of Wisconsin Press, 1961) explores the topic of taboos and other attitudes to animal foods in the Old World.
[34] Fickeler, "Fundamental Questions," in *Readings in Cultural Geography,* pp. 114-15.

and eating of monkeys because they resemble people. There is an ancient and now nearly universal taboo on the eating of human flesh, although cannibalism itself has often had a religious basis.

Geographically significant food taboos pertain to pigs and cattle. Having different religious bases, they have opposite effects on the land. Pig's flesh is forbidden to Jews and Muslims and to all but the lowest Hindu castes, because it is considered ritually unclean; it conveys pollution.[35] This makes the handling of pigs taboo also and pigs are not raised.

Now, in most peasant societies, pig raising is a cheap economic activity in a mixed crop and livestock system, requiring little capital or energy. In the cork-oak region of Spain and Portugal, the pig is essentially a forest animal. This cheap source of food—there are 8,000,000 pigs in the Iberian peninsula, or roughly 21 per hundred people—is missing in the similarly forested Atlas Mountains across the Strait of Gibraltar, because the people there are predominantly Muslim. In the eastern Mediterranean, because of centuries of Muslim rule, pigs are not even kept by the Christian population of Lebanon, although they could be raised there and in Turkey, Syria, and Israel, as they once were.

Where Islam has taken hold in tropical Asia, it has driven out pig eating and pig keeping. The largely Christian Philippines has over 6,000,000 pigs, or 30 per hundred people, twenty times higher than the ratio in dominantly Muslim Indonesia. The ratio would be much higher were it not for the pig raising Indonesian population of pagans, Christians, and Chinese. Muslims in Southeast Asia rigorously avoid pork. It was once a preferred food and a festival specialty, as it still is among non-Muslims. But because of the taboo, Muslim Malays no longer keep pigs. Agriculture in Chinese villages in Malaya is characterized by the intensive cultivation of vegetables, in which pigs play an integral role: vegetable mash and other wastes are fed to pigs, which are raised for human food, while returning fertility to the soil in the form of manure. This successful tropical ecosystem is absent in adjacent Malay villages.

The taboo on beef in Hindu India and in most Buddhist countries differs from the pork taboo. The beef taboo is a refinement of the concept of *ahimsa,* which imposes a general prohibition on the taking of animal life, and has, for historic reasons, emphasized the sanctity of the life of the cow.[36] In contrast to the pork taboo with its resultant absence of pigs, the beef taboo in India is associated with an enormous cattle population, a large part of it aged, diseased, and unproductive. Able stock breeding is rare, producing an inefficient working cattle population, ostensibly kept to supply draught power and milk. Many Western writers and Indian secularists have advocated improving Indian agriculture by changing Hindu attitudes toward cow slaughter. References by such writers to the custom as a superstitious worship of the sacred cow discloses basic misconceptions. *Ahimsa* is one of the nobler religious concepts, and technological reformers realistically ought to control cattle overpopulation under the conditions imposed by the acceptance of the *ahimsa* ideal. For

[35] Both Hinduism and Judaism emphasize the contrast between things, especially foods, that are ritually pure (Hindi: *pakka;* Hebrew: *kasher*) and those that are ritually impure (Hindi: *kachha;* Hebrew: *taref*).

[36] See W. Norman Brown, "The Sanctity of the Cow in Hinduism," *Bulletin of the Institute of Traditional Cultures,* XXVIII (1957), 29-41.

example, the rigorous control of breeding among cattle in India might be expected to bring remarkable benefits.

As in Malaya, sharp ecological contrasts appear in India among religious groups with different food patterns. Pigs are uncommon in Hindu as well as Muslim villages, but they abound in Christian and tribal ones, where they may be seen snuffling along the lanes and rooting in the surrounding brush, incidentally playing a useful role as village scavengers. The contrast in food habits has spatial effects as well. As the pig is considered defiling by Hindus and Muslims, a tendency exists for these two religious communities to segregate themselves from the others in order to avoid pollution. This may produce, or at least reinforce, the desire of each group to live apart. A self-segregating tendency of this kind is an element of the ghetto phenomenon (see Chapter 5).

Less explicit differences in food consumption, having less obvious consequences, may also be associated with different religious traditions. The different fish consumption patterns in Hindu India and medieval Christian Europe provide an illustration. The Hindu taboo on fish, especially sea fish, varies a good deal from region to region. Even Brahmans are permitted to eat fish in Bengal, although elsewhere they are usually strict vegetarians. Nevertheless, a considerable part of the Hindu population abstains from fish, and the fishing trade is universally given a low social rating. Even today, Indian fisheries remain in need of capital and sound management, but the respectable business castes are reluctant to have anything to do with them. In the long run, Hinduism has penalized Indian fishing.

In Catholic Europe, on the other hand, the practice of abstaining from meat on Fridays, but not from fish, was a persistent stimulus to the enlarging and extending of sea fishing operations during the Middle Ages. In their efforts to provide salted and marinated fish for Friday eating throughout the year, fishermen and seamen such as the Scandinavians and Bretons explored the northern seas in the fifteenth century. A place of respect had been given to fishermen in the New Testament—Christ said to them: "Follow me and I will make you fishers of men" [37]—and the fish was a symbol of early Christianity. In contrast to Hindu society, medieval Christian society encouraged and subsidized fishing.

Even among communities of the same religion, there may be notable contrasts in consumption patterns. Within Buddhism, the reluctance to kill cattle and eat beef diminishes in areas distant from its hearth. Beef cattle production in Japan has been inhibited in the past, but more recently, even Buddhist priests have been accustomed to eat beef. De Planhol quotes a proverb to the effect that two Muslims travelling abroad together stay thin, but one Muslim alone grows fat (on forbidden foods). [38] Pig raising is uncommon among the Jews in Israel, although at least nine in ten American Jews ignore the pork taboo.

Asceticism is an ideal that creates its own laws regarding the consumption of certain foods. Several Protestant denominations, such as the Methodists and Baptists, prohibit the taking of alcohol, which is also taboo for

[37] Matthew 4:19.
[38] Xavier de Planhol, *The World of Islam* (Ithaca, New York: Cornell University Press, 1959), p. 57.

Muslims and high caste Hindus; some frown on the smoking of tobacco, which is also banned in the Sikh religion; and the Mormons add coffee, tea, and kola drinks to these. The Muslim inhibition of grapevine cultivation except for the limited production of table grapes and raisins is particularly noticeable in the same Mediterranean littoral areas where pigs are absent.

WORK TABOOS. Some religions prohibit work on certain occasions and some find objections to certain forms of economic activity. Both kinds of work taboo affect the way the land is used. Our secular work week, with a day of rest on Sunday, originated in the first kind of taboo. The Jewish *Shabbath*, whatever its origins in the Babylonian calendar, was a day consecrated to God and in that sense was transmitted to Christianity, which in time changed the day of sabbath observance from Saturday to Sunday. The development of rapid communications and such integrating institutions as international banking in the nineteenth century thoroughly secularized and internationalized the Christian work week, particularly at the government level. But in non-Christian rural areas, where production and marketing patterns are still not tightly bound to the administrative and commercial rhythms of the cities, Sunday is not a day of rest and has no special character. The Muslim Friday, *yaum al-jum'a* or "day of assembly," does not have the character of a sabbath, and normal economic activity is not completely suspended as in traditional Christian lands. Orthodox Jews, on the other hand, rigorously observe the sabbath work taboo, refraining also from many purely domestic activities. Such observances entail serious disruptions in a complex society and economy. They are a distinctive feature of contemporary life in Israel, where a thoroughgoing application of the sabbath idea has a correspondingly disruptive effect.

Most ancient ethnic systems, including the Chinese, Indian, Babylonian, Mayan, Greek, and Roman, employed sacred calendars which contained an array of feast days having a pronounced taboo character.[39] Their whole ritual and profane life was fixed to these dates, which occurred with great frequency in some religions. In ancient Egypt one-fifth of the year consisted of sacred days on which work was prohibited, while in republican Rome, one out of every three days was "unlucky," and much normal activity was discouraged.[40] Like these, the Hebrew sabbath was a consecrated taboo day.

A rigorous sabbath observance must have been out of place among the pastoral Hebrews, since a nomadic herding people could hardly function effectively under such a regime, especially at certain critical seasons. This dysfunction may account for the absence of the sabbath concept in Islam, which permits work for the provision of the family on Fridays.

In the religion of simple agricultural societies, the taboo days that require rest from work are usually geared to a lull in the cycle of agricultural work or to moments when an important phase of activity is initiated

[39] Friedrich Heiler, *Erscheinungsformen und Wesen der Religion*, Vol. I of *Die Religionen der Menschheit*, ed. C. M. Schröder (Stuttgart: W. Kohlhammer Verlag, 1961), p. 153.
[40] Bouquet, *Comparative Religion*, 6th ed. (Baltimore: Penguin Books, Inc., 1962), p. 50.

or terminated. In tribal societies that lack a religious calendar, certain days are consecrated on an *ad hoc* basis and may be marked by a strict taboo on normal work. The practice is common among tribal peoples, where Christianity has not displaced it, in Southeast Asia and Oceania. Among the isolated Mentawei people, on the island group some distance from the south coast of Sumatra, the ritual taboo on work, called *punen*, occurs quite often. In addition to *punen* for planting, harvesting, and other agricultural operations, there are *punen* for marriages and for deaths in the village, *punen* for building a new house, and *punen* for the outbreak of disease.[41] So many *punen* might be prescribed annually among some Southeast Asian pagan peoples that European administrators thought it contributed significantly to low agricultural productivity. However, most of these occasions would naturally fit into the agricultural cycle without disrupting it. Exceptions would be the unforeseen emergencies, such as disease and death, when work would cease anyway.

It is evidence of cultural blindness that Europeans should have been unhappy with these flexible schedules while maintaining a routine program of weekly rest periods. While a calendar is essential for a civilization, its value for agricultural operations is likely to be exaggerated. Apart from a few observations of the sun and the stars, the man working the land can be guided by the annual biological cycle, even close to the equator where there are no significant seasonal changes in temperature or length of daylight. About the Zande, African cultivators who live just north of the equator, de Schlippe writes: "The correct sowing seasons of the various crops are known to the people not according to months and dates but according to their observations of stars and wild life—vegetation, animals, insects. . . . [These ecological 'symptoms'] represent an accumulation of experience used intuitively by the older people, who are unable to formulate them in words, perhaps even in conscious thought." [42]

The elaboration of sacred calendars, often the work of ritual specialists in an urban environment, may seriously interrupt the rhythm of farming and herding. Through the first Christian millennium until recently, the Church in Southern Europe came to regulate agricultural life, prescribing times of sowing and harvesting within rather narrow limits. As numerous obligatory feasts of saints were added to the calendar, interruptions of a rather arbitrary kind in addition to the Sunday sabbath were imposed by the Church on the optimum work cycles of agriculture and of urban craft and commerce. In France in the fourteenth century, there were forty-two of these feasts, which with Sundays and Easter, meant a rigidly scheduled suspension of economic activity on about one day in four in the course of a year. Religious direction of the agricultural work cycle thus affected the rate of energy input in the exploitation of the land. It may also have helped to perpetuate archaic agricultural systems. Perhaps for this reason, new crop patterns associated with an improved agriculture were adopted late in the productive Paris Basin and parts of Catholic southern Germany.

Some religious systems impose taboos that restrict choices regarding

[41] E. M. Loeb, *Sumatra: Its History and People*, Wiener Beiträge zur Kulturgeschicht und Linguistik, III (Horn-Wien: Berger, 1935), pp. 167, 183.
[42] Pierre de Schlippe, *Shifting Cultivation in Africa: the Zande System of Agriculture* (London: Routledge & Kegan Paul, Ltd., 1956), p. 152.

resource use and create traditions that inhibit economic activity, even after the religious sanction has weakened. A tribal group in friendly contact with others may become economically specialized as a unit, perhaps in order to maintain a clear identity. Often such arrangements become sanctified by ritual. In the Nicobar Islands, only one community was permitted to make canoes and trade them to the other groups, all of whom used canoes. For the other groups, canoe making was ritually taboo. Among some tribes in India, Arabia, and Africa, ironworking is a specialized craft practiced by individual families who are not of the community, but belong to a diffuse kin group of smiths, essentially a caste. The caste specialization does not persist so much because the smiths have a private technical knowledge as because smithing, for the nonsmiths, is often ritually taboo.

This pattern is seen at its most elaborate in the unique caste arrangements of the Hindu religious social system. Each caste in the traditional Hindu system has its own set of moral obligations, or *dharma*, an element of which is the caste's prescribed economic function. With increasing secularization, only a small minority of caste members in certain castes now follow the traditional occupation. Nevertheless, in the Hindu world, economic activity in the past has been controlled and channeled to a large extent by the religious system.

Concepts of *ahimsa* and ritual pollution affect the social ranking of a caste's function and thereby the interrelationships among economic activities. Occupations like fishing are penalized on religious grounds and inhibited in their development by their consequent separation from sources of capital, enterprise, and technological stimulation. Tanning, leatherworking, and seafaring are other examples. Soldiering, like seafaring, has been neglected in areas where castes having these functions have been absent, as in Bengal. Even agriculture, the basic Indian economy, has suffered. It is not the business of a Brahman to cultivate land, so that where circumstances have obliged Brahmans to take up farming, they are ideologically and psychologically out of place. Some business and trading castes refrain from agriculture and never acquire enough interest in its workings to put it on a sound basis.

Some agricultural societies in Southeast Asia evince a prejudice against mining, even of gold; they believe that the removal of ores offends the earth spirit. In other tribal religions, the earth is thought susceptible to desecration in other ways. The Baiga, a people of the Central Indian jungles who cultivate with the digging stick, consider the use of the iron-shod plow an abomination because it tears the breast of the earth mother. In the American Southwest, government agricultural advisors who tried to introduce early spring plowing among the Indians of Taos ran into a wall of hostility; the Taos believe that in spring the earth mother is pregnant and must be treated delicately.[43]

In India, a religious objection to any form of agriculture is found among the Jains. Underlying this is the prohibition against taking animal life. Since plowing and other agricultural activities must destroy some insect

[43] Edward T. Hall, *The Silent Language* (Greenwich, Connecticut: Fawcett Publications, Inc., 1959), p. 79.

life, these activities are taboo for certain Jain sects, necessarily members of a stratal religious system with a very high concentration in towns.

The prohibition on usury imposed in the past by both Catholicism and Islam has had important geographic consequences. This measure tended to freeze capital, restrict credit, and encourage specialized communities outside the faith to engage in moneylending. Despite the church ban on lending at interest, banking and the granting of loans as business credit rather than consumer credit evolved in northern Italy and southern France in the late Middle Ages, spreading northward to Flanders. The prohibition was finally discarded in the European lands that became Protestant after the Reformation. After that, and perhaps because of it, the rapid rise of the North Sea mercantile nations occurred. At the same time, the Mediterranean and Middle Eastern lands suffered from economic stagnation. Credit institutions are still defective in these traditionally Catholic and Muslim countries.

Indirect Expression of Religion on the Land [44]

Since most religions have something important to say regarding reproduction, life and death, they may affect the demographic component of the population-resources equation. Some religious concepts encourage high birth rates. The biblical injunction to "be fruitful and multiply" is taken in Judaism to be a directive to marry early and raise a large family, a directive evidently not followed by all but the most orthodox, since Jewish birth rates in contemporary Western societies are quite low. In Hinduism, it is considered immoral by most castes for a woman to die before she has been married or for a man to die without sons. This religious attitude would not permit the condition of prolonged bachelorhood and spinsterhood found in both Catholic Ireland and Lutheran Sweden, which makes for a low rate of population increase, noteworthy in the case of Ireland because of the Catholic prohibition of artificial contraceptives. The Hindu desire for a child early in life encouraged early marriage, which resulted in a high maternity rate among younger women. This has been counteracted by the religious sanction that forbids the remarriage of widows; young widows of older husbands are eliminated as potential mothers.

Societies at various times have tried to check growth rates by such techniques as female infanticide, induced abortion, and the use of contraceptives. As religious concepts permit or forbid such techniques, demographic consequences are bound to vary. Japan has recently been able to reduce its population growth rate drastically only because contemporary Japanese religious systems are quite permissive regarding techniques forbidden to Roman Catholics.

While the prohibition against taking human life is general among most of the major religions, it is not consistently interpreted. The different intrinsic value placed on all human life by different religious systems can be seen in their attitudes to war as an instrument of religious policy, rang-

[44] Zimpel's article on the impact of religion on the landscape of the eastern Mediterranean is a valuable model for this kind of study. *Mitteilungen der Geographischen Gesellschaft in München*, XLVIII (1963), 123-71.

ing from the prescribed use of "holy wars" to the Buddhist pacifism of Asoka, who renounced war altogether. The demographic consequences of these different philosophies have had significant effects on the land.

Since the Hindu-Buddhist-Jain systems consider all animal life sacred, they may have encouraged the conservation of wild life and forest habitats. The Hindu ideal may be expressed in faunal distributions, in the pattern of wild and settled land, and in the nature of pioneer Hindu settlement in forested areas.

Examples of direct conservation effected by simple religions are known. Groves were the primary sacred places of the early Indo-Europeans and the older agricultural folk of the eastern Mediterranean; sacred groves on hilltops were cut down as abominations by the still pastoralist Hebrews on their entry into Canaan.[45] Taboo forest areas were widespread in tribal Indonesia, India, and Africa,[46] but some of the pagan people who had maintained such protective "green-belts" quickly destroyed them after conversion to Christianity.

There are many ways in which religious ideas condition social and economic behavior and thereby affect the land. In an agricultural ecosystem, for example, productivity may be in part a function of inputs of labor. Variation in inputs of labor may in turn be related to differences in religious and cultural values. Thus in traditional India, the patterns of capital formation and investment and the levels of labor input and consumer demand may be related in some way to the Hindu-Buddhist theme of world renunciation.[47] The task of the geographer is to identify the patterns of behavior, expressed in such forms as quanta of labor input, that have operated on the land and, perhaps, to make out the guiding values behind such patterns of behavior. For example, one might compare attitudes to certain resources among pioneer settlers of different denominations as they moved westward across North America, as Bjorklund has done for the Dutch Reformed community in Michigan.[48]

Different religions require different allocations of resources and energies for the maintenance of institutions. The monastic life is such an institution, one fundamental to Buddhism, since it is the monastic community which lives the truly Buddhist life. Monastic life has a similar role in the Eastern Orthodox Church. In Catholicism, the life of monks and nuns has been supported as a pious alternative to "living in the world" although there has been a progressive shift by the Catholic monastic population in the direction of "working in the world."

The economy of monasticism differs according to these different levels of withdrawal from the world. In Buddhism and Jainism, it has been

[45] Fickeler, "Fundamental Questions," *Readings in Cultural Geography*, p. 113.

[46] H. H. Bartlett, "Fire, Primitive Agriculture, and Grazing in the Tropics," in *Man's Role in Changing the Face of the Earth*, ed. William L. Thomas (Chicago: The University of Chicago Press, 1956), pp. 710-11.

[47] Cf. the large literature by sociologists and economists on the question of the relationship between the Protestant (Calvinist) ethic and the rise of capitalism and industrialism in western Europe and North America. A related sociological question is the extent to which the behavior of a religious group derives directly from its religious beliefs or, alternatively, from its historical experience as a social community. See Gerhard Lenski, *The Religious Factor: a Sociological Study of Religion's Impact on Politics, Economics, and Family Life* (New York: Doubleday & Company, Inc., 1961), based on a study of metropolitan Detroit.

[48] Elaine M. Bjorklund, "Ideology and Culture Exemplified in Southwestern Michigan," *Annals*, Association of American Geographers, LIV (1964), 227-41.

unusual for monks to work at mundane tasks, including agricultural ones, although Japanese Zen Buddhist monks are an exception; in Catholic monasteries, active programs of work have usually been followed, sometimes with marvelous results—Chartreuse liqueurs and the Mendelian genetic rules, for example. A geographic evaluation of monastic institutions should ascertain how much, if at all, an agricultural economy is handicapped when monasteries own much of the cultivated land. It should estimate how much society loses when a part of the most energetic age-classes chooses to be celibate, and, if Buddhist, to be economically unproductive. Would this always be a loss? Might not the monastic institution act to stabilize population, making the accumulation of productive capital easier? Answers to these questions might qualify the negative judgment that history has rendered on monastic institutions.

An accounting of monastic institutions should also consider the services they provide. In a Buddhist civilization, the monastery is the chief mechanism of integration, as the church is in a Christian civilization or the school in a secular one. In the traditional Theravada Buddhist system, the experience of monastic life enjoined on all males provided most of the young men with a brief period of training in a literary tradition. This approach to mass education was possible because the monasteries were supported by villages close by, and in return provided this indoctrination and certain ritual services. A notable consequence is the high literacy rate among such predominantly rural peoples as the Burmese and Thai.

Religious systems which oblige the individual to read scriptures create favorable conditions for attainment of a high literacy rate. The Jews of the Diaspora have encouraged mass male literacy and have prized the intellectual skills required to interpret religious law. Islam, as an equalitarian, universalizing system, might also appear to require full male literacy but has not insisted on this. Perhaps because the urban environment of early Islam provided facilities for oral instruction of the public by literate speakers, religious institutions producing mass literacy have not appeared in Islam as they have in Judaism and Theravada Buddhism. Protestantism requires individual knowledge of the gospel in one's native tongue. Soon after the Reformation, Protestant communities, particularly the Calvinists, attained a high literacy rate, which played a role in the subsequent rapid economic growth of northern Europe. This Protestant requirement, combined with missionary aims, has also spurred an intense effort to translate the scriptures into other languages and to create written languages for the purpose where none existed before in many parts of the non-European world.

Many traditional religious systems have institutions which provide social welfare services, at varying cost to society. When the social services provided through a religious institution cost much more than they are worth, society is wasting some of its resources. A malfunction of this kind seems to have occurred in the Islamic institution of the *waqf*.[49] The *waqf* is an endowment of properties and businesses, interest and earnings from which support many social services for the needy, while maintaining various religious institutions. Although satisfying welfare needs, the

[49] See the article "Wakf," in *Shorter Encyclopaedia of Islam*, ed. H. A. R. Gibb and J. H. Kramers (Leiden: E. J. Brill, 1953).

waqf contributed to the stagnation of Middle Eastern agriculture, because restrictions were placed on the disposal of endowed lands. The land was poorly used and undertaxed, and technical innovations were inhibited. Little more than fifty years ago, the *waqf* properties in the Ottoman Empire amounted to three-quarters of all arable land in the state. Since then, legislative reforms in most Muslim countries have tried to put *waqf* land into circulation as private property in order to stimulate improvements on it.

Islam has sought to define and regulate the entire political, economic, and domestic life of a society through its sacred law, *sharī'a*, and the *waqf* is only one of many Islamic institutions which have put their mark on the land.[50] Because the urban milieu was preferred for the full Islamic life, agriculture was adversely affected by the removal of potential sources of capital and initiative from the producing land. One writer has argued that Islam may have inhibited agriculture more directly: "The 'Oral Traditions' of Islam are filled with a spirit hostile to the peasantry."[51] Islam prescribes rules of inheritance requiring land and other property to be divided equally among sons, with daughters receiving smaller portions. This has resulted in excessive fragmentation of agricultural land, with a corresponding decrease in agricultural efficiency.

Women in the Islamic world have usually been completely shut off from the life of religion, neither learning the scriptures nor participating in the services of the mosque. The Islamic tradition has segregated women and thus has deprived them of many of the economic functions they perform in other societies. Work in public view is especially discouraged. In both East and West Pakistan, as a rule, Muslim women do not work in the fields, whereas in many Old World societies, women are involved in such agricultural tasks as planting, weeding, and harvesting. Muslim women do not convey produce to market, nor do they engage in selling it. In most Muslim cities, women do not even shop in the bazaars for their own household needs. These arrangements represent one disposition of a society's economic energies, arrangements that in this case have grown out of the values and social institutions of Islam.

Religious Landscapes

Do the institutions of a given religion, acting with varying intensity on the land, combine to produce a cultural landscape that can be identified surely as a religious one? The spires of churches in Christian lands are only a single element linking evidently diverse landscapes whose molding forces have been technological and ecological rather than spiritual. By such indices as the varying ratio of unit cult structures to population, the landscape may tell something about the relative intensity of religious expression at different times and in different places.[52] Some cultural landscapes are more religious in appearance than others, while some religious systems may be more effective than others in the morphogenesis of

50 See de Planhol, *World of Islam,* especially pp. 1-70.
51 *Ibid.,* p. 42. Even trade and commerce, which are specially favored in some Koranic verses, are hampered by archaic controls exerted by the traditions and the canon law. See Zimpel, *op. cit.,* p. 163.
52 Zimpel, *op. cit.,* pp. 123-24.

cultural landscapes. When the concept of religion is extended to comprise a society's modal value system, the connection between belief and action is strengthened, and cultural landscapes may express an ideological *Gestalt*. The industrial town and the state socialist farming commune, for example, exhibit layouts and structures which are products of the religious geographic concepts of a secular age.[53]

The expression of formal religious systems on the land is always more conspicuous when a common environment is occupied by two or more locally dominant systems. One may cite the Christian landscapes in Lebanon or the Muslim landscapes in southern Yugoslavia and Albania. In the United States, certain denominations and sects that exercise a strict regulation of social and economic behavior have created distinctive, religion-imbued cultural landscapes. The Amish Mennonite ("Pennsylvania Dutch") communities of southeastern Pennsylvania are one example. The absence of separate church structures, the lack of finery and display, the reluctance to use motor vehicles, the exclusivist rejection of other social and material traits of neighboring non-Amish communities are elements of behavior and attitude based on religious principles that are strongly expressed in the Amish landscape. Such cultural particularism is often the mark of an ethnicizing subsystem of a universalizing religion.

In the mid-nineteenth century, the Mormon religion also developed certain cultural attributes which have given the Mormon country in Utah and parts of Idaho, Wyoming, Arizona, and New Mexico its character of a distinctive religious landscape.[54] Under the guidance of a religious hierarchy that for a while maintained a true theocracy, the Mormon settlement was built as a religiously inspired representation of the City of Zion, with square blocks, wide streets, fields bordered by Lombardy poplars, frame churches of unpainted cedar, and a compact arrangement of irrigated land around the nuclear settlement.

A recent study of another cohesive American religious community demonstrates the intimate connections between religious ideology, social behavior, and cultural landscapes. This is Bjorklund's study of a Dutch Reformed community,[55] numbering about 40,000, in southwestern Michigan. It shows how the principles of the Dutch Reformed religious subsystem were applied in a new area of settlement where space had to be organized and resources exploited. Over a period of a century and more, choices and decisions based on firm religious beliefs have produced a landscape containing these features: church-centered nuclear settlements, in which retail and commercial services are kept to a minimum and deliberately placed on the periphery rather than in the center; compact tracts of land owned by church members, making it possible to exclude undesirable aspects of non-Calvinist life from the Dutch Reformed living space; specialized types of commercial agriculture, an outgrowth of doctrines demanding self-reliance and productive activity; local light industries, established for the same reason and intended to engage energies in

[53] Isaac, "The Act and the Covenant: the Impact of Religion on the Landscape," *Landscape,* IX (Winter 1960), 18.
[54] Donald W. Meinig, "The Mormon Culture Region: Strategies and Patterns in the Geography of the American West, 1847-1964," *Annals,* Association of American Geographers, LV (1965), 191-220; Lowry Nelson, *The Mormon Village* (Salt Lake City: The University of Utah Press, 1952).
[55] *Op. cit.,* pp. 227-41.

the winter off-season and even to supplement the day's work on the farm during the agricultural season; church-operated primary and secondary schools with religious instruction and a work-oriented curriculum; Dutch place names, but little else of Dutch character in the landscape, illustrating the nonethnic character of the religious system, which, finding Dutch cultural elements unwieldy in the American context, dispensed with them. Studies such as this point to new directions which cultural geographic research can take in pursuing the theme of man's modification of his environment.

CHAPTER 4

CHAPTER *the religious organization*
of space

Sacred Space and Sacred Territory

Some societies follow what appears to be a sacred pattern in transforming earth space. In this process, various kinds of sacred space may be distinguished and delimited. Just as ecology is selectively ritualized in the simple ethnic religions, so are sacred places and territories in such religions a selective sanctification of tribal geography. Aboriginal Central Australian collecting bands ritualize their living space through the medium of ancestor-myths, landmarks associated with the sacred ancestors, and sacred ritual objects (*churinga*), presenting a stylized picture of the tribal territory. This is the circulation field suggested by the location of sacred places and of the ancestral tracks made in the "dream time." [1] The Australian aborigine's tribal world is "made a cosmos," in Eliade's words, by being ritualized; beyond is chaos. If the strong religious ties with the land are severed, the tribe may disintegrate.[2]

The mythical geography of the Australian aborigine's "dream time" corresponds to the geographic setting of the living tribe. Some religions have mythical or sacred geographies that do not correspond so closely to reality. Nevertheless, the topography of Paradise, the Garden of Eden, Valhalla, the Elysian Fields, Hades, Hell, and other such constructs of the religious imagination all seem to involve a sacralization of some elements of terrestrial geography.

Ritualization of local territory, often the village territory, is also found in technologically more advanced societies. Christianized Indian villagers in Chiapas, the southernmost highland of Mexico, go annually in a procession conducted by lay officers to each of the sacred landmarks that de-

[1] Ronald M. Berndt, "The Concept of the Tribe in the Western Desert of Australia," *Oceania*, XXX (1959), 98-99.
[2] Kaj Birket-Smith, *Primitive Man and His Ways* (New York: New American Library [Mentor Books], 1963), p. 28.

limit the village lands. The ceremony is thought to preserve the social institutions and sacred geography of the pre-Spanish Mayan culture.

An actual demarcation of the ritualized village space takes place periodically among both Hindu peasants and tribal folk in southern Asia. The villages of swidden cultivators in Southeast Asia are separated ritually from the outside world during taboo periods marked by animal sacrifice. A ritual quarantine is imposed, no one being allowed in or out of the village. In various ways a space is distinguished that differs in its ritual properties from the surrounding territory—obstructions are placed on paths to the village, symbolic barriers of thread may be run across streams and along slopes.

Some peoples maintain an open sacred space, intended for ritual acts, within the otherwise profane village territory. In the Polynesian religions, this taboo area was set outside the village living space to prevent its being inadvertently contaminated and desecrated. The Greek temple began as such a demarcated ritual space, and the open altar of the Temple of Heaven in Peking is a refinement of the same concept. The earliest Islamic prayer space, the *muṣallah,* was a demarcated open space.

In Hinduism, sacred or ritualized territory exists at several scales. For the exorcism of disease, especially in northern India, the village is the ritual area. The caste territory, a closed field of circulation and interaction, is barely discernible in the distribution of castes, but is made explicit in caste rules. Certain castes impose a penalty on members, especially women, who cross the caste's territorial boundaries. About 500 B.C., the middle Gangetic Plain was the ritually pure Brahman homeland, while the deltaic lands of Bengal to the east and the Indus Valley to the west were *mlechha,* polluting alien territories. It was improper for a Brahman to travel there; he had to perform penance and purifying ceremonies on his return. The concept, extended south through the peninsula, has helped to define the Hindu homeland. Even recently, certain respectable castes have performed penance after journeys across the ocean, while first sons born abroad may still be taken back to the pure land of India for their first ritual haircut.

The national territory appears as ritually pure in other ethnic religions. The Jewish concept of a sacred land, Zion, is well known; that no other land could be ritually proper is suggested in the exiled poet's question: "For how can we sing the Lord's song on alien soil?" [3] Shinto holds that a special guardianship is extended to the land and people of Japan by the ancestral deities,[4] and the "sacred fatherland" is a fundamental concept in modern nationalist quasi religions.

It would appear that formal sanctification of a homeland reduces mobility. At one level of the Chinese religion, the sacred foci are the ancestral graves. Because some, if not all, family members were obliged to maintain these, mobility in the past should have been significantly reduced. It does appear that large-scale migration within China has occurred only in catastrophic circumstances. The sanctity of the ancestral place was so strong in the last century that bodies of Chinese who died

[3] Psalms 137:4.
[4] D. C. Holtom, *Modern Japan and Shinto Nationalism: a Study of Present-Day Trends in Japanese Religions,* rev. ed. (Chicago: University of Chicago Press, 1947), p. 13.

overseas in Southeast Asia were shipped home, guarantees to this effect often being written into labor contracts. In Vietnam, where the same tradition occurs, peasants in the crowded Tongking delta in the past century were extremely reluctant to abandon ancestral graves to move to the undeveloped lands of the Mekong delta despite the excellent agricultural opportunities created there by the French. Roman Catholic Vietnamese, liberated from the ties of an ethnic religion, were much more mobile, just as the Christian population of Europe has been rather footloose compared to the sedentary Chinese.

The Christian example shows that the practice of burial need not be associated with strong attachment to place, while Hinduism shows that the practice of cremation can be. Although Hindus are often bound by social obligations to a geographically fixed community, they may forsake home at the approach of death in order to be cremated at some sacred spot, preferably at Banaras, where their ashes can be cast into the sacred Ganges. Muslim pastoral nomads bury their dead and mark the grave in a simple manner, but they have little attachment to a fixed place. Shia Muslim cultivators in Iraq and Iran, often tied to a particular piece of land, have preferred to be buried away from home near one of the great Shia shrines.

SACRED PLACES. Within a group's ecumene, particular places may be associated with a manifestation of sacred power. The sacred may be generalized in trees, rocks, hills, lakes, and grottoes, or may appear specifically in places associated with some sacred person or event. Sacred power can be attractive, making the place a shrine, or terrifying and repellent, making the place taboo and even accursed, forbidden to all with the possible exception of protected ritual specialists.[5]

Since perception of the sacred varies from group to group, one can hardly generalize about the principles of sacred location. Regionally, however, cultures have tended to assign sanctity to different categories of natural objects, such as certain species of trees in tropical Africa, or high places in the ancient Near East.

The geography of Indian sacred places is made complex by a variegated pantheon and by several geographic levels of sanctity. Most Hindu holy places are landmarks rather than places sanctified by the mythological or historical acts of a hierophant, although this type of sacred place is also known. Important Indian holy places are found at river sources (Lake Manasarowar, Amarkantak), at river mouths or confluences (Sagar Island, Allahabad), at physiographic breaks in the courses of rivers (Hardwar, Srirangam), on peaks and hilltops (Mt. Abu, Mahabaleshwar), on headlands (Cape Comorin, Rameswaram), and beside lakes, in caves, and occasionally in association with natural curiosities.

The distribution of Hindu holy places thus shows some correspondence with selected features of the physical landscape, although the degree of holiness ascribed to such features varies from region to region. The sanctity of places is diffuse enough to be significant in the location of Hindu temples. Since most large Hindu temples are endowed as autono-

---

[5] The ambivalence of sacred power, which may be helpful or harmful, appears in the Latin word *sacrum*, the root of "sacred." *Sacrum* has the double sense of "holy" and "unholy," both of which are to be differentiated from "profane."

mous institutions by persons of wealth, these structures need not be very close to communities, although especially sacred sites create their own population clusters providing a variety of economic services. The choice of temple site is thus adjusted to the local sacred geography, and Hindu temple location is to that extent god-oriented rather than community-oriented.

The location of churches, mosques, and temples in the universalizing religious systems is not exclusively oriented to communities. Sometimes they sanctify legendary or historical events. Sites connected with the lives of teachers and saints frequently acquire a sacred character in both Buddhism and non-Protestant Christianity. In Islam, the common people often venerate tombs of reputed holy men and build mosques nearby, despite orthodox disapproval.

In Catholic Europe, some churches were built to incorporate or dominate the pre-Christian sanctity of such sites as tops of hills in France and Italy. When sending a mission to evangelize England in the sixth century, Pope Gregory is said to have suggested that the mission should not demolish the pagan temples but should transform them into churches. A thousand years later, the Spaniards in the Americas did destroy pre-Christian temples but sanctified their sites by building churches on them; most of the scores of churches in and around the Mexican town of Cholula are built on mounds that once supported Aztec temples.

Such a transference of sanctity is common. In the early Islamic period, some churches and Zoroastrian temples were converted into mosques, following "the rule that sacred places survive changes of religion." [6] When one religious system does not completely displace another, both may share the holiness of a particular place. In the Middle East and India, the same place may be venerated by two or three different religious communities for its supposed association with the folk hero of each.

THE RELIGIOUS CENTER. Sacred places become religious centers as simple ethnic religious systems evolve into more complex ones. The religious centers, which become the primary foci of sanctity, may supplant the diffuse sacred places of the preceding simple religions, or they may merely supplement them.

The role of the earliest religious centers in the evolution of urban life is still not clear and was probably not the same everywhere. The Celtic peoples of pre-Roman Britain had religious centers which functioned as the sites of annual religious and political gatherings, but these centers were not urban places marked by permanent dwellings. The Mayan culture did have agglomerations of permanent buildings at such places as Uxmal and Chichen Itza, but it is thought that these were purely ritual foci, perhaps not permanently inhabited, so that the town may never have appeared indigenously. In Hindu India, however, towns have often grown around sacred places and their temple structures and this process may throw light on the relationship of religious centers to urban beginnings. Once the idea of the town is established, the sequential relationship between religious function and other urban functions may be reversed. The tutelary gods of Greek cities were merely the household

[6] "Masdjid" in *Shorter Encyclopaedia of Islam,* ed. H. A. R. Gibb and J. H. Kramers (Leiden: E. J. Brill, 1953).

gods of some prominent city family, the god being adopted, with somewhat expanded divine functions, while the family remained as hereditary caretakers.[7] The expansion of systems like Catholic Christianity and Islam into lands not previously urbanized provided the impulse to town formation around religious centers. The church in northern Europe from the sixth to the ninth century and in Hispanic America in the sixteenth, seventeenth, and eighteenth centuries created religious centers which were at the same time centers of both urbanizing and civilizing processes.

The role of religious centers in different religious systems and the circumstances of their growth follow no set pattern. Religious centers which are purely sacred foci should be distinguished from those which are organizational centers or religious capitals. Allahabad, Banaras, and contemporary Jerusalem are religious centers primarily because of their intense sanctity of place, while Jerusalem in the first millennium B.C., Rome, Kyoto, and Salt Lake City are examples of religious capitals, although previous sanctity may have inhered in some.

Most large cities that are religious centers are functionally diversified and have had the opportunity to become so for geographic reasons not directly related either to their sanctity or to their role as religious capitals. Jerusalem during part of the first millennium B.C. was the capital of both the ethnic religious system and the state. It had its counterparts in cities like Babylon and Thebes, centers of ethnic religious systems and the capitals of states in the ancient Middle East. Tenochtitlan and Cuzco, respective centers of the Aztec and Inca empires, were first of all centers of ethnic religious systems which extended their sway by a religious justification of warfare. The Aztec poet-priests institutionalized warfare as the essential source of human sacrifices needed for the worship of the sun.[8] Thus the religious capital became the center of an imperial military network. Peking during the last millennium has functioned jointly as political capital of imperial China and the administrative center of the official religion.

Among religious centers which are also moderately large cities, Mecca and Medina are today almost unique because their religious role constitutes their predominant urban function. They are religious centers because of their association with Muhammad and the birth of Islam, Mecca also retaining its pre-Islamic sanctity as the site of the megalithic Kaaba. Mecca and Medina were at that time trading towns on the caravan routes linking Yemen and Ethiopia with the Fertile Crescent by way of the Hejaz, but this functional significance disappeared long ago. With a combined permanent population of about 300,000, the two cities exist as such today because they are the sacred cities of Islam and the objects of an annual pilgrimage which all male Muslims are enjoined to perform at least once. But Mecca was not a religious capital, having been abandoned as the seat of the Caliph, the head of the Islamic community, shortly after Muhammad's death.

Some intensely sacred places have never developed as urban centers,

[7] N. Fustel de Coulanges, *The Ancient City: a Study on the Religion, Laws and Institutions of Greece and Rome,* 10th ed., trans. Willard Small (Boston: Lothrop, Lee & Shepard Co., Inc., 1901), pp. 164-65.

[8] H. R. Hays, *In the Beginnings: Early Man and His Gods* (New York: G. P. Putnam's Sons, 1963), pp. 536-37.

although they may be repositories of wealth and artistic skill. Ise, recognized as the hearth of Shintoism, Mt. Abu, the chief shrine of the Jains, and Delphi, the most sacred place in the classical Athenian world, are examples. Their lack of growth can be related in part to their situation and site. Such foci may have a sanctity originally based precisely on the mystery and wonder of a remote place. At some like Mt. Athos and Ise, urban agglomeration has been deliberately restrained by reserving the site for religious specialists. Such isolated shrines may nevertheless have symbolic significance as centers of political integration. The Oracle of Delphi, according to Deffontaines, was one of the principal elements of Greek unity.[9]

PILGRIM CIRCULATION. A religious center has particular geographical importance because of the strong centripetal flow of traffic it may generate. A circulation system is set up that may augment significantly the flow of traffic in existing patterns; or it may cut across other circulation patterns associated with commercial, administrative, and military networks. This religious circulation promotes secondary flows of trade, cultural exchange, social mixing, and political integration, as well as certain less desirable flows, such as the spread of epidemic diseases.

The *hajj*, the annual Muslim pilgrimage to Mecca, exemplifies the purely religious circulation that has little relation to other primary circulation patterns. The *hajj* is remarkable for its very large source area, extending from Senegal to Celebes, for the importance of the event in the lives of the participants and for the isolated situation of the sacred focus. In recent decades, the annual total of pilgrims has fluctuated widely with varying political and economic conditions. A crudely estimated average of the traffic would be 100,000 pilgrims a year.[10]

The demands of the *hajj* traffic have been met in the past century by the development of modern transportation networks. Steamship services link East Africa, India, Malaya, and Indonesia with the Arabian port of Jidda; a short-lived pilgrim railway was built from Damascus to Medina; and there has been a proliferation of international flights between Jidda and most Muslim countries. The older caravan and sailing ship routes, while carrying a much smaller volume of pilgrim traffic, nevertheless kept in motion over the centuries a vast internal circulation of Muslims that must have served as a valuable link between different regions. This is reflected in the cosmopolitan character of the permanent population of the two holy cities. Although exclusively Muslim, this population is for the most part not of local Arabian origin.

Pilgrim circulation has been an important feature of the geography of Hindu India.[11] Sanctity of place being geographically diffuse, the volume of pilgrim traffic to a particular holy place is partly related to ease of transportation and population density in the hinterland. However, the level of sanctity of a particular place, endorsed by holy men and ascetics, is related primarily to the sacred topography of Hindudom rather than to the distribution of population.

[9] *Géographie et religions* (Paris: Gallimard, 1948), p. 311.
[10] This suggests that the injunction to make the pilgrimage at least once in a lifetime can be fulfilled by no more than one male Muslim in fifty.
[11] Agehananda Bharati, "Pilgrimage in the Indian Tradition," *History of Religions*, III (1963), 135-67.

There is an informal hierarchy of district, regional and pan-Indian pilgrim circulation. Several important foci of pan-Indian pilgrimages mark approximately the limits of the Indian religious homeland: Cape Comorin and Rameswaram are situated at the southern extremities of the Indian peninsula, Badrinath and Kedarnath are located in the Himalayas near the source of the Ganges. Over the centuries, the major holy places of India have drawn a part of their pilgrim traffic from all over the Hindu realm.[12] This primarily religious circulation created and sustained bonds of place that gave rise to the idea of India as the Hindu homeland, and this idea has in turn been transmuted into modern Indian nationalism.

Pilgrim circulation has also been a feature of the Japanese religious system and the Shinto gods themselves are taken on an annual pilgrimage to their ancestral home. Pilgrimages have been relatively unimportant as a medium of inter-regional circulation in China, despite the presence there of a Buddhist religious stratum. Pilgrimages have been of secondary importance for community-building in Buddhism and Christianity, which have had other organized networks, monastic or ecclesiastical, to sustain an internal circulation. After Buddhism was displaced from its hearth in the eastern Gangetic Plain early in the Christian Era, the potential foci of world Buddhism, the sacred sites associated with the life of Gautama, remained dormant for centuries. Pilgrim and monastic circulation was intraregional rather than pan-Buddhist. Now that a Buddhist ecumenical movement is developing, the holy places of the Buddhist hearth like Gaya and Sarnath are once more functioning as Buddhist centers, despite their situation in a non-Buddhist region.

In medieval Christendom, the church network provided a more effective circulatory system than pilgrim traffic flows. Considerable pilgrim traffic developed around regional foci like the shrine of St. James (Santiago) in Compostela, Spain. Some of these, like Canterbury and Reims, sanctified by historical events and by their role as early regional centers of ecclesiastical administration, became "national" shrines, Canterbury becoming in time the sacred focus of the Anglican Church. Islam, too, has its regional pilgrim circulation, especially among the Shia, who add pilgrimages to the holy cities of Kerbela in Iraq and Meshed in Iran to the Meccan *hajj*. A regional circulation may thus produce regional integration within a wider religious system. The shrine of the Virgin of Guadalupe near Mexico City has been the popular sacred focus of an ethnically mixed Mexican Catholic population since the sixteenth century, the centripetal flows it has stimulated complementing the network of religious orders and secular clergy centered on the adjacent capital.

Sacred places, such as the shrine of Guadalupe, that appear to develop spontaneously are characteristic of the Indian and Roman Catholic worlds. They are associated with specific manifestations, attracting masses of pilgrims because of this. The sanctity of such places is informally acknowledged in the Hindu world, while requiring validation by the Church in Catholicism, but in neither case are the reasons for the great popularity of certain pilgrim resorts clear. It has been suggested that the phenomenon of Guadalupe took hold precisely because some integrating symbol was needed at that particular historical moment to provide the

[12] On one recent occasion, an estimated two million pilgrims assembled at one site, far outnumbering the largest *hajj* assembly at Mecca.

new Mexican population with an identity of its own, and in this the Virgin of Guadalupe has been eminently successful. But what of popular Catholic shrines like Lourdes, Fatima, Lisieux, Loretto, Paray-le-Monial, and Ste. Anne de Beaupré? The social and psychological springs which motivate pilgrimages to these places are outside our field of investigation, but their geographic characteristics can be studied and have been. The great volume of Catholic pilgrim traffic is striking. Ste. Anne de Beaupré on the Quebec coast has two million visitors a year; Lourdes in southwestern France and Lisieux in Normandy receive well over a million. These numbers are made possible by the size of the Catholic populations in adjacent regions and the rapid and relatively cheap transportation provided by railroads and buses, so that within France, at least, the regional variation in the flow of pilgrims to these centers does not seem to be significantly related to the distance-cost factor.[13] Despite these large flows and the sanctity ascribed to these places, the towns themselves have only a few thousand residents.

Some religions, such as Judaism and most American Protestant denominations, have hardly any secondary religious foci. Judaism as a displaced ethnic religion has its primary sacred focus at Jerusalem, and its more generalized sacred hearth in Zion, or the Land of Israel (*Eretz Yisrael*).

Weakly developed religious centers do appear in Protestantism. Geneva has a special attraction for Calvinists, but it can be treated as a religious focus perhaps only if the definition of pilgrimage is broadened to include various contemporary forms of tourism having a rather diluted religious motivation. Pilgrim travel to religious shrines has often had the character of tourist travel and recreation. In the Orient as in the West, there is now also a largely secular tourist traffic to places of religious significance that have some historical, architectural, or scenic interest as well.

CULTURAL AND COMMERCIAL CIRCULATION OF RELIGIOUS SYSTEMS.   Another religiously motivated circulation, important in the diffusion of ideas within a religious realm, is that organized around religious study centers. These may be foci of centripetal flow when an administrative network is not well developed. In Buddhism, lacking such a network, the great monastic centers of learning in northern India, such as Nalanda in Bihar, could attract scholars from places as distant as northern China during the early Christian centuries. On a smaller scale, the Jewish communities of the Middle East during the same period participated in a scholarly traffic focusing on the Talmudic schools in Mesopotamia.

Without a priestly class and a hierarchical spatial organization, Islam had a similar intense development of scholarly circulation. Because Islamic ideology penetrates so many aspects of life, the study of religious scriptures is related to the study of the law and thence branches into history and science. The major Islamic study centers from the seventh century were thus early universities, usually located in the principal mosque of large cities. Fez, Bokhara, Cordoba in Moorish Spain are towns whose chief significance to Muslims is the contribution of their schools to the Islamic cultural tradition. Cairo is renowned as the seat of Al-Azhar

[13] Deffontaines, *op. cit.*, p. 305.

Mosque and University, the pre-eminent institution of Muslim learning today.

Centers of religious and secular study also functioned as growing centers of intellectual circulation in seventeenth and eighteenth century North America, with the establishment of schools like Harvard and Princeton by the Congregational and Presbyterian churches, respectively, in order to provide for the training of clergymen.

A type of circulation partly focused on religious centers is the trade in commodities needed for ritual in religious institutions or in the home. When travel was slow and difficult, the demand for sacred or ritually necessary objects of small bulk could play an important role in stimulating and maintaining long-distance trade. The demand for ritual goods still produces some curious trade patterns, as when conch shells by the hundreds of thousands are gathered each year by Muslim divers in the vicinity of Ceylon for the preparation of articles used in Hindu temple and domestic ritual in Bengal. Sandalwood as incense in Oriental rites has stimulated the commercial penetration of remote tropical forests, having at one time led to frenzied exploitation in places as far as Timor and Hawaii.

After Christianity became the official religion of the Roman Empire, a trade in the aromatic gums used for incense in Mediterranean churches extended to the shores of the Arabian Sea. The aromatic resins, frankincense and myrrh, could stand the cost of caravan transportation to the Mediterranean from the wooded highlands of South Arabia and Somalia. This trade in Christian ritual goods, still moving overland between Yemen and the Mediterranean in the seventh century, was part of the traffic which sustained the prosperity of Mecca and Medina. An important byproduct of this circulation may well have been the Arabian contact with Christianity, which contributed to Muhammad's creation of a new religion. Other circulation systems associated with pilgrimages and trade in sacred goods have probably carried a similar freight of significant religious ideas.

Territorial Organization of Religious Systems

Geographically separate communities of the same religion are connected in various ways to form organized religious territories. The spatial structure of religious systems would seem to have significance for their fluidity and dynamism, for the circulatory traffic they generate, for their ability to foster regional identity, and for the nature of their interactions with other religious systems.

The church that prescribes a common ritual and liturgy for separate communities of the same religion is a familiar organizational form. The union of individual communities required for the training of ritual specialists, for agreement on the modification of ritual, for transmitting common traditions, and for financing the building of new cult units is an element of the spatial structure of a church. Integration of religious communities may also take place outside the formal institutions of a church, through lay bodies, for example, or through the medium of persons who perform religious functions although not delegated or appointed to do so, such as the individual missionary in Muslim society.

Some religious systems are less organized than Christian ones and do not constitute churches. The spatial organization of these systems comprises the lines of connection among all sorts of religious practitioners and personalities as well as their relationship to the community. Religious specialists range from the shaman and prophet through the mystic, saint, and ascetic, to the priest, the religious teacher, and the minister.

Thus, a tribal religious system in which the shaman is the chief religious personality is organized quite differently from one, such as the priestly religion of the ancient Celts, which requires the intensively trained ritual specialist. Not that a highly ritualized religion calls for a special priestly class. The Hopi religion with its complex and highly formalized ritual is operated by the instructed community, there being no Hopi priests. Hinduism has several different kinds of religious functionary, all important in the religious life of Hindu India, and each exhibiting a different pattern of spatial organization. The hereditary ritual specialist, the Brahman, represents one of these types.

The religious community comprises both laymen and religious specialists, but the latter sometimes form a separate organized community concerned with living a religious life. Buddhism, Jainism, the defunct universalizing religion of Manichaeism, and, to an extent, the Greek Orthodox Church are systems in which the truly religious life is or was considered to be that of the congregation of monks. The arrangement of Manichaean society on the basis of aptitude for the religious life was clearly defined: there were the "Elite" or "Perfect," who abstained from marriage, the eating of meat, the ownership of property, and all forms of secular work, and the "Listeners," who had only to follow the Ten Commandments. In such cases, the spatial organization of the monastic community may become the critical element in the maintenance or expansion of a religious territory.

AUTONOMY AND HIERARCHY. Spatial structures of religious systems range between the poles of self-sufficient local autonomy and fully centralized hierarchy. The tension between these two positions is evident in several religions. Locally autonomous systems may seek more secure organization, at least in some facets of their operation, while centrally organized systems are frequently challenged by movements aspiring to an independent religious life. Cultural contact among different systems encourages such trends. For example, traditional Judaism of the Diaspora has not had a church organization, but it is presently acquiring the institutions of a church, particularly in America, where it is almost expected to. In Japan, non-Christian religious groups have begun to resemble churches through contact with Christianity, while on the other hand some Japanese Christians, attuned to the loose organizational structure of traditional Oriental religions, have founded a "non-church movement" within Japanese Christianity.[14]

Freemasonry appears to be a substitute for church hierarchy and ritual

[14] Werner Cohn, "Is Religion Universal? Problems of Definition," *Journal for the Scientific Study of Religion*, II (1962), 31.

in some Protestant societies. This is a universalist ethical system that complements the Church, not least in providing a complex ritual and an elaborate territorial hierarchy. It is particularly opposed by the ritually elaborate and hierarchical Catholic and Lutheran churches. Mormonism manages to combine in a remarkable way the desire for a democratic religious community, characteristic of the environment out of which it arose, with Freemasonry's ritual and hierarchical organization.

The tendency of organized churches is "to channel or suppress manifestations of religious experience," [15] and religious communities seeking autonomy in Western Christianity, like the Albigensians (Cathari) and the Anabaptists, have often come into conflict with the established church. Contemporary movements in both the Protestant and Catholic churches of the West are trying to create more vital religious communities than those already in existence, with opportunities for other than rigidly institutionalized religious experience. Some movements do not go unopposed. In America, the unconventional religious behavior called *glossolalia,* or "speaking in tongues," has recently stirred controversy within the Protestant Episcopal Church. The diffusion of *glossolalia* illustrates the different levels of spatial organization within religious systems. The channels of diffusion along which this novel form of religious experience is communicated are hardly those of the administrative and financial network of the Episcopal Church.

In some religious systems, informal circulation networks may be the most important, if not the only, mechanism of spatial integration. This is pretty much the case in Hinduism, which is exceptional in considering the quest for personal religious experience and knowledge and the exercise of religious charisma to be the highest forms of religious activity. Such activity does not meet serious opposition from Brahman ritualists. The pervasiveness of this attitude towards religious experimentation is one of the distinguishing and, at the same time, unifying features of the Hindu religious complex. In the United States, where organized religion is popularly given high value, religious experimenters are likely to be looked at askance.

A useful index in locating religious systems on the continuum between local autonomy and a centralized territorial hierarchy is the degree of ritual self-sufficiency accorded to the local community. Muslim and traditional Jewish communities are ritually self-sufficient. Their autonomy is not complete because some aspects of religious life, such as religious education or interpretation of the law, may be entrusted to specialists (*mullah, rabbi*), who may come from outside the local community. The community normally remains free to accept or reject such specialists who are not indispensable to its religious life. Moreover, the specialists themselves are not territorially organized in a hierarchy.

In some Protestant denominations, ritual self-sufficiency and even considerable autonomy in doctrinal matters may go together with efficient financial organization of wide scope having such objectives as the support of missionary activity or the publication of religious literature. With laymen participating in the management of church business, such denomi-

[15] Max Weber, "The Social Psychology of the World Religions," in *Theories of Society: Foundations of Modern Sociology,* II, ed. Talcott Parsons *et al.* (New York: The Free Press of Glencoe, Inc., 1961), p. 1400.

nations as the Baptists, Congregationalists (now the United Church of Christ), Unitarians, and Quakers have the character of religious cooperatives, with each member community retaining its autonomy in ritual and liturgical matters.

LOCALLY AUTONOMOUS RELIGIOUS SYSTEMS. The locally autonomous community occurs among all types of religion, from simple ethnic to universalizing. Simple ethnic religions are with few exceptions locally autonomous. The common religious personality is the shaman, "the oldest religious specialist in the world." [16] This is a man or woman who is a member of the local tribal community, usually not a shaman by heredity; as shaman, he or she may well be the person of chief influence in the group. Priests intensively trained in an oral tradition may appear even when writing and urban life are absent. Among the British Celts, nonhereditary priests were trained at special centers, the Druidic disciples having to travel over long distances. Such a religious system is incipiently national rather than tribal.

Locally autonomous organization may be retained in the simpler forms of national religion. In urban Greece and in Rome, the early city cults were outgrowths of family rites and did not require a hierarchical priestly structure. Only after the introduction of the eastern mystery religions did a specially trained priestly class appear, exclusively occupied with religious functions and set apart from the community.

A stratified priesthood need not be organized in a territorial hierarchy. In ancient compound ethnic systems, the city or state cult with its managing priestly class might be found at a single center. The centralized ritual performance, such as the exclusively imperial rites in China, would serve vicariously for the provincial and rural population, who might perform supplementary local and domestic rites. Priestly Judaism in Solomon's time was something like this and Solomon's temple, it has been suggested, was in effect the king's private shrine.[17]

Territorial hierarchies of religious specialists were found in some ancient states and empires. The official Inca religion was maintained by an organization parallel to the secular administration. For the Mayan culture, there is evidence that assemblies of calendar priests from different culture areas were held periodically in the chief cult place.[18] But the spatial structure of a religious system need not correspond to local economic organization or administrative structure: local autonomy is quite common in compound ethnic religious systems. Before universalizing religions appeared, religious organisms seem to have been less dynamic and less mobile than economic and political organisms.

Local autonomy occurs in a complex ethnic or universalizing religious system if individual communities adhere to a common program provided by a sacred written or oral authority. Even the individual communities of a dispersed ethnic religion can thus maintain common religious institutions and practices for a long time. This has been true of Judaism since

[16] Hays, *In the Beginnings,* p. 529.
[17] Heinz-Gerhard Zimpel, "Vom Religionseinfluss in den Kulturlandschaften zwischen Taurus und Sinai," *Mitteilungen der geographischen Gesellschaft in München,* XLVIII (1963), 131.
[18] Hays, *op. cit.,* pp. 469, 497.

the destruction of the temple and its priestly hierarchy. The common sacred program has been provided by the Old Testament and the volumes of scholarly commentary on it. By following this program, a quorum of ten adult males can constitute a fully functioning religious community of Jews, and the rabbi, a teacher and legalist, is not needed to perform ritual.[19] In the performance of ritual, individuals thought to be of the ancient priestly family (*kohen*) have a minor, unessential role, rather like vestigial Brahmans. Apart from this, the idea of a hierarchy is quite foreign to Judaism.

In these circumstances, religious institutions carry a relatively low maintenance cost, and each Jewish community can be practically a self-sufficient religious community. Intermittent social and intellectual contacts among Jewish communities in different regions have perhaps been instrumental in maintaining the surprisingly high degree of uniformity that characterizes Judaism despite its wide dispersal. The Jews of Yemen, preserved as such by their own attitudes and those of their Muslim neighbors, are exceptional in having experienced many centuries of isolation from Jewish society in other lands. Elsewhere, isolation has led to the absorption or radical transformation of Jewish communities, some of mixed descent. Such partly or almost completely assimilated communities are the Chinese "Jews" of Kaifeng, the "Black Jews" of Cochin in southwestern India, the Bene Israel of Bombay, the Falasha of Ethiopia, and the Khazars of the Caucasus, now extinct.

Local ritual autonomy characterizes Hinduism. Religion rationalizes the caste society, and much religious ritual is performed within a caste context. Many low castes and those arising from sects, like the Lingayats of Mysore, provide their own ritual specialists. Most castes, however, require and can obtain the ritual services of Brahmans. The identification of Brahmans as priests may be misleading, as no religious organization unites the Brahmans of different communities, let alone different regions. In most Hindu communities, hereditary Brahman ritual specialists (*purohit*), native to the place, serve the local population. The sacred program they follow is transmitted locally from father to son, and normally they do not change their place of residence and service.

Here and there, the sanctity of a place, the concentration of population, or the patronage of rich men and rulers, might lead to the growth of assemblages of temples and their Brahman caretakers. The rites performed at such sacred places merely supplement the religious services provided in one's own place of residence and among one's own caste. Thus each local Hindu community follows its own religious practices or sets of practices, supplementing them by ritual observances associated with a pilgrim circulation.

This pattern of local autonomy in formal religious practice is by no means the whole of Hinduism. There are also numerous widely diffused philosophic and religious movements, both ancient and modern, many seeking to transcend caste. They are transmitted by the circulation of audiences who will travel far to listen to a particular religious teacher —who need not be a Brahman—and by the circulation of wide-ranging

---

[19] In some eastern European communities, the rabbi was also something of a wonder-working holy man, a mystic and sorcerer.

ascetics and other holy men who live on alms and are well regarded by the people.[20] The great pilgrim assemblages such as the Kumbh Mela, held every twelve years, also provide a regular opportunity for the exchange of religious ideas among many different kinds of Hindus. This circulation of religious ideas has moved with apparent freedom across language barriers. Perhaps this is because Hindus have been especially receptive to the communication of religious thought; the language of religious discourse has been the unifying common language of Hindudom. A profusion of autonomous, caste-related cults, overlaid by several different kinds of religious circulation is, then, the grossly simplified spatial structure of the diverse, internally dynamic, yet almost wholly unorganized system called Hinduism.

Among the universalizing religions, Islam and some forms of Protestantism are characterized by locally autonomous religious communities. Islam resembles Judaism in insisting that every male member of the community can and should participate equally in all ritual aspects of religion. Although the mosque is a place of public worship, prayer itself often has a private and autonomous character.

Islam's instructions are simple and explicit in many respects, but its extended comments on social and economic life have produced several schools of legalists who are the most important religious specialists in Islam. The traditional religious program provides for the maintenance of these and other institutions having more than a local purpose. Usually, the Islamic state with its bureaucratic machinery has served as administrator of such institutions, in the absence of a church. Islam does not make a direct levy on individuals for the maintenance of religious institutions and the relief of the unfortunate, but it does prescribe a substantial charitable contribution from those who can afford it. Traditionally, this is assessed at 2½ per cent per annum of one's net worth. When strictly followed, this humanely intended commandment must have frustrated economic growth. Nevertheless, the welfare institutions it fostered, particularly those assisting the traveler, made possible free circulation within the Muslim world. Anywhere within this world, a Muslim could feel at home among his fellows.[21] Despite the absence of a religious hierarchy and a formal religious organization of territory, separate Muslim communities are linked by strong ties, maintained by common institutions and an active circulation. Individual communities maintain themselves by providing a universal training for their members in at least the basic ethical and ritual requirements of Islam. While cultural and political conflicts among Muslim peoples have been common, Islam has never experienced the degree of devolution toward separate subsystems that has occurred in Buddhism and Christianity. Indeed, considering its numbers and areal extent, the Islamic world community, the 'umma, exhibits a remarkable uniformity and cohesiveness.

Specially organized communities have appeared in Islam under certain circumstances. Intermittent warfare with Christianity in the Mediter-

---

[20] The characteristic Indian religious behavior of withdrawal from the world, which such persons manifest, is usually unorganized.

[21] The extensive Asian and African travels of the scholar Ibn Battuta in the fourteenth century demonstrate the wide range of movement that was then possible for an authority on Islamic jurisprudence.

ranean fostered Muslim counterparts to the Christian military-religious orders. At present, bourgeois brotherhoods and ascetic orders like the Sanusi are hierarchically graded systems that have contributed vitality to Islam, especially in North Africa. They intensify the commitment of the urban population to the Islamic ideology and supply energies to missionary activity.

PROTESTANT DENOMINATIONS—AUTONOMOUS AND HIERARCHICAL. American Protestant denominations made up of locally autonomous communities have the form of organization called congregationalism. Major denominations of this kind are the Baptists, the Disciples of Christ, and the (former) Congregational Church. Extreme forms of congregationalism are found among such smaller groups as the Quakers, Unitarians, and Amish. These locally autonomous denominations differ from Islam and Judaism in not adhering rigidly to a common ritual and liturgical program. On the contrary, the precise form of worship among Baptists, for example, is a matter of local congregational choice, as is the provision of religious specialists, local churches choosing and ordaining ministers.

Even in congregationally organized denominations, ministers are specialists needed to perform key rituals and to exercise, in however diluted a form, spiritual authority as pastors for the care and protection of souls. In this role, they continue a fundamental and distinctive Christian institution. Congregationalist denominations have widely different requirements for the training of ministers, with noteworthy consequences. Baptist churches increased much more rapidly than Congregational churches during the last century partly because Baptists aspiring to be ministers were given much briefer training than Congregationalists.

The spatial structure of congregationalist denominations is usually weakly developed. There are conventions of representatives at the district, state, and national levels, but resolutions passed at these are not binding on member churches. The Quakers (Friends) are distinctive in seeking broad democratic consensus through regular meetings with other groups in the same district and region.

Progressively more hierarchical and more tightly organized spatially are denominations having presbyterian and episcopal systems of organization. The Presbyterian churches have a form of board government, with ministers and elected lay members serving on governing boards. There is a territorial hierarchy ranging from local units (sessions) through presbyteries and synods, which govern large regions, to the General Assembly; ministers are ordained by the presbytery. The environment of American political institutions has had its effect on denominational organization, leading to the partial adoption of presbyterian features by a number of other American denominations.

The episcopal system, used by the church of that name, by the Lutheran churches, and by the main body of Methodists, represents a modification of the Roman Catholic hierarchical model. In the United States, these churches allow local congregations more control and choice than do the parent systems in Europe. The spatial organization of these churches is also less rigid than in the old Christian lands of Europe. Parish territories and their equivalents do not regulate an individual's choice of a church, so that churches are free to develop service areas with fluid boundaries, much like retail stores and shopping centers. Some denominations have created planning bodies to advise about the optimum location of new churches and ways to maximize their services to highly mobile communities. Methodist churches owed some of their great success in the last century to a flexible organization of frontier land in circuits, where several local communities could be served by a lay preacher. Today, Methodist and other Protestant denominations are trying to develop patterns of organization adapted to contemporary forms of urban life. The "supplementary service church," operating in a predominantly nonresidential area and maintained by a centralized denomination, is one such current experiment in the spatial organization of religious systems.[22]

Whatever their system of church organization, most major Protestant denominations have shown an ability to organize for a variety of church-related purposes. For missionary activity, even the most congregationalist denominations effect some central coordination. The support of activities by contributions from the membership harks back to the tradition of the tithe, the contribution of a tenth of one's income, an obsolescent Jewish custom which was carried over into early Christianity and thereafter maintained and enforced by the Church. The sums raised by Protestants have gone into extensive building, education, and welfare programs, in addition to missionary work, with much left over for various business investments. Annual contributions to Protestant denominations in the United States alone are currently estimated to be close to $3,000,000,000. This cooperative financial activity linking many local communities is a vital aspect of the Protestant church organization of space.

HIERARCHICAL RELIGIOUS SYSTEMS. Some Oriental religions have organizations resembling a church, without the requirements of exclusive membership that most Christian systems impose. A spatially interconnected body of ritual specialists is found in the state cult of imperial China, popular Taoism, Shinto, and most forms of Buddhism. These priestly corps differ from Brahman ritualists in having some formal spatial organization. Also, except for Shinto priests and some high-ranking Taoist ones, they are not hereditary.

These Oriental systems vary considerably in the development of territorial hierarchies. The official Chinese cult was plainly hierarchical: the rites permitted in a given town were graded according to the administrative rank of the place and were performed by the resident government officer. But the spatial organization of Theravada Buddhism consists of rather tenuous regional associations of monasteries. Each monastic center supplies a small, indeterminate territory with the services of monks as resident or peripatetic ritualists.[23] The service area of a monastery is thus a virtually autonomous local hierarchy. Vertically, this hierarchy is weak, since high rank need not have corresponding disciplinary power.

[22] See Manfred Stanley, "Church Adaptation to Social Change: a Typology of Protestant City Congregations," *Journal for the Scientific Study of Religion,* II (1962), 64-73.

[23] That Buddhist monks have come to serve as ritualists, in addition to leading a prescribed religious life and providing religious education, negates an original aim of Buddhism, which was to eliminate the need for ritual specialists from Indian life.

Monastic networks of communication may penetrate, inform, and manipulate a largely rural society, as shown by the emergence of the Buddhist clergy as a political force in Ceylon and Vietnam.[24] In Ceylon, however, the apparently homogeneous field of communication among Buddhist clergy is affected by the Sinhalese caste system, so that, quite contrary to the intentions of early Buddhism, different castes have come to predominate in different monastic orders.

An elaborate vertical and territorial hierarchy occurs in certain ethnicized or segmental religions, apparently as a defense mechanism against change or competition from more powerful religious systems. Such structures are always in danger of rapid ossification. The Lamaistic version of Buddhism, which prevailed in Tibet and Mongolia, departs from the Oriental pattern of weakly organized religious systems in having a well-developed hierarchy. In recent decades, one of the new Oriental religions, the Cao Dai system of South Vietnam, has deviated in the same way by copying features of the Roman Catholic hierarchy. The neoethnic Druze religion also arose out of a loosely organized Islam and developed a rigid hierarchy as a means, perhaps, of self-preservation.

The phenomenon of Mormonism presents a similar contrast between the democratizing forms of American congregationalism out of which it evolved and the elaborate, though broadly based, ecclesiastical hierarchy that is the Church of Latter-Day Saints. While authoritarian, the hierarchical structure defers to the congregationalist tradition by involving most of the participating Mormon society from adolescence up as graded religious-social functionaries, becoming what O'Dea calls "a democracy of participation and an oligarchy of decision-making and command." [25] Mormon society is an age-graded religious society with an additional sequence of grades based on religious or organizational aptitude, and thus it resembles both Freemasonry and the ancient mystery religions, such as Mithraism. The Mormon hierarchy culminates in a board and president who have authority over the entire church.

In contrast to American Protestant denominations, the Church of Latter-Day Saints has a precisely laid out system of territorial organization. Settled Mormon territory is organized in wards, a ward being the equivalent of a parish and having ideally a population of about 750. Wards are grouped in stakes, supervised by a cleric of higher rank but much smaller than the Catholic or Protestant diocese, having on the average a population of about 5,000. The boundaries of these ecclesiastical units are carefully delimited, and in areas of rapid population growth are frequently redrawn in order to maintain the desired quota of population in each unit.

Intensive participation in church affairs by laymen with some local initiative, complemented by far-reaching supervision by the Church, results in a remarkably activist religious society. The intensity of Mormon ecclesiastical circulation has no equal in other religious systems. Apart from visits of inspection from the center, representatives from almost

[24] See, e.g., David E. Pfanner and Jasper Ingersoll, "Theravada Buddhism and Village Economic Behavior: a Burmese and Thai Comparison," *Journal of Asian Studies*, XXI (1962), 341-61.
[25] *The Mormons* (Chicago: University of Chicago Press, 1957), p. 165.

every Mormon community are required to attend a conference in Salt Lake City twice in each year.[26] A full tithe levied for the maintenance of the Church makes it affluent, while its dynamism is partly a result of a two-year universal training required of young males in the form of mission work in non-Mormon territory. Mission lands having a growing population of Mormons are organized territorially in districts and branches. These universalizing agencies of Mormonism extending abroad do not obscure one of the elements making the Church of Latter-Day Saints a unique American religious system. It is the only church which has organized, fully and almost exclusively, the territory of a true religious homeland in the United States.

Of the older hierarchical Christian churches, the Eastern Orthodox Church has a less marked separation of clergy from laity than the Catholic Church. Local communities have some say in the choice of bishops and, as in early Christianity, in related matters of church administration. The laity even shares in decisions on doctrinal matters. The Eastern hierarchy also differs from the Catholic one in having no supreme authority equivalent to the Pope. Like the Nestorian and Monophysite Christian churches before it, the Eastern Orthodox Church may have evolved into distinct though intercommunicating ethnic churches partly because it did permit a degree of local autonomy. This tendency to form distinct regional bodies may have made Christianity more vulnerable to absorption by Islam in the territories of the Oriental churches.

SPATIAL STRUCTURE OF THE ROMAN CATHOLIC CHURCH. The Roman Catholic Church has been described as the "most formidable religious institution in the history of the world." [27] The Church is responsible for organizing communities of Roman Catholics, teaching the faith, providing ritual services, and regulating the morals of the faithful. The personnel of the Church is hierarchically organized for these purposes, and the earth space over which the Church extends its influence is systematically organized in ecclesiastical administrative units. The Catholic Church is by far the most extensive—and also the most ancient—spatially organized system in the world today.

The Catholic Church extends a network of administration and of religious service, at different levels of intensity, over most of the inhabited portion of the earth's surface.[28] Areas of pioneer missionary activity, sparse and widely scattered settlement, limited resources, or difficult communication are organized as missions, prefectures, and vicariates, in an ascending order of territorial integration. Fully organized space containing self-supporting Catholic communities is known as the "ordinary hierarchy" and is divided into dioceses.

The diocese has traditionally required an urban nucleus for the headquarters or see (i.e., seat) of the administrative officer, the bishop. The

26 Donald W. Meinig, "The Mormon Culture Region: Strategies and Patterns in the Geography of the American West, 1847-1964," *Annals,* Association of American Geographers, LV (1965), 215.

27 Jaroslav Pelikan, *The Riddle of Roman Catholicism* (New York: Abingdon Press, 1959), p. 12, cited in Edwin S. Gaustad, *Historical Atlas of Religion in America* (New York: Harper & Row, Publishers, Inc., 1962), p. 111.

28 It does not do so in effect now because of the objections of some Communist governments.

territorial hierarchy of the Church in fact grew out of the organization of the Roman Empire, with each recognized urban place requiring a bishop, at least in the long civilized Mediterranean lands. This reflects the significance of urban cells in early Christianity; the contrast between Christianized town and unconverted countryside is preserved in the term "pagan," its root being the Latin *pagus*, a rural district.[29]

To a degree Catholicism, like Islam, requires and fosters the town. The agglomeration of settlement has sometimes been part of a planned program of Christianization, as in the Augustinian and Jesuit mission program in Spanish America, which created many quasiurban nuclei, the *reducciones*, or "settlements." [30] Other forms of organization have sometimes been more effective. The Celtic Christian abbeys of Ireland were far more influential in spreading and sustaining Christianity than the decadent territorial hierarchy, largely because the Irish were dispersed and tribally organized, in contrast to the population in the former provinces of the Roman Empire.[31] But where the town-based hierarchy developed successfully, it provided avenues of recruitment from the hinterland and paths for cultural impulses from the center that have constituted the circulatory system of a civilization.

The diocese is the essential unit of the territorial hierarchy, but not the smallest. The diocese is divided into parishes—the Greek root of the word meant "neighborhood"—each under the care of an ecclesiastical officer, the priest, who is responsible to his bishop. In dominantly Catholic countries in Europe, where the ecclesiastical structure is old and elaborate, the diocese may contain several hundred parishes, but abroad, the average density of the parish net drops to 100 parishes to the diocese in Anglo-America and 40 in Latin America.[32]

Several dioceses, about four on the average, comprise an ecclesiastical province. This is under the general supervision of an archbishop, who has also the responsibility of a bishop for one of the dioceses in the province, called the archdiocese.[33] The authority of archbishops over bishops is primarily administrative, whereas a bishop has both administrative and spiritual authority over the parish priest. Some dioceses, especially in Italy, are exempt from archiepiscopal supervision. The regional administrators and ritual specialists—the bishops and archbishops—are subordinate to the Pope, who is himself the Bishop of Rome, which is called the Apostolic See or Holy See.

The pattern of Catholic territorial organization is based on certain geographic principles, but historical changes and special circumstances in some regions have modified these. The spatial principle on which the parish unit is based is that the parish population must be able to fulfill

---

[29] The same Latin root gives us via Late Latin and Old French the word "peasant."

[30] By 1767, the Jesuits had established 38 of these in Paraguay, with a population of 106,000 Indians. See Kenneth S. Latourette, *History of the Expansion of Christianity*, Vol. III (New York: Harper & Row, Publishers, Inc., 1939), p. 155.

[31] M. W. Heslinga, *The Irish Border as a Cultural Divide: a Contribution to the Study of Regionalism in the British Isles* (Assen: van Gorcum, 1962), p. 113.

[32] Anglo-America contains, for statistical convenience, the predominantly Catholic French-speaking part of Canada.

[33] "Diocese" is here used, unless otherwise indicated, as the generic term for the territorial unit represented by both dioceses and archdioceses, regardless of administrative status.

its obligation to attend Sunday mass at the parish church. Traditionally, therefore, the parish has been only a few square miles in area, and in the old Catholic lands of Europe, this pattern has long been established, with the number of Catholics per parish priest generally falling under one thousand.

This standard has been modified in New World lands, often of sparse and dispersed rural population. This has called for expedients like the Brazilian church-hamlet, occupied only on weekends by the population of outlying ranches or coffee estates.[34] In general, the parish area has increased in non-European lands.

There is, however, one broad region which shows a remarkably large and consistent departure from the territorial organization of the Catholic Church as found both in Europe and in many non-European lands, such as the United States and India. The region comprises the former colonial empires of Spain and Portugal. Here, five to ten times more Catholics must be served by each member of the territorial clergy than in Spain, Portugal, and most Catholic countries. The ratios of Catholic population per priest are 915 for non-Communist Europe, 730 for Anglo-America, and 4,950 for Latin America (Fig. 4).[35]

This regional deviation cannot be related primarily to sparse population. It may be that the region is too poor to support a more intensive service network or that the Church exhibits a lack of initiative inherited from the period when it was managed as the Royal Patronage of the Indies.[36] This particular dispensation placed most of the administration of the Church under the usually benevolent but often constricting control of the Iberian monarchs for almost three centuries. As at that period, European clergy still dominate the Church in parts of Latin America; even in this century, many secular priests are Europeans. Finally, most Latin American governments have opposed the Church at one time or another in the postindependence period. However, the underdevelopment of Catholic institutions in Latin America, especially in rural areas,[37] clearly goes back to the colonial period. In the 1650's, a Portuguese Jesuit was appalled by conditions in Brazil; churches and priests were far too few, and episcopal supervision was entirely inadequate; many Portuguese did not go to Mass throughout the year and few observed the holy days.[38]

The other departure from the traditional European parish standard occurs in the large industrial conurbations. In Europe, the growth of these cities has meant that the parish is less and less able to serve its Catholic population, especially in the new suburbs. French cities like Paris and Marseilles have more than 2,000 Catholics per diocesan priest, with the highest ratio, 3,600 per priest, occurring in the suburban diocese of Versailles. On the other hand, the dioceses having about 500 Catholics per

[34] Deffontaines, op. cit., pp. 147-48.
[35] Sources of statistical data in this section are: Annuario pontificio per l'anno 1963 (Vatican City: Tipografia poliglotta vaticana, 1963); National Catholic Almanac, 1964, ed. Felician A. Foy (Paterson, New Jersey: St. Anthony's Guild, 1964). "Catholic population" is as defined in these sources.
[36] Latourette, op. cit., Vol. 7, p. 167. See also the statement "The Church in Latin America," National Catholic Almanac, 1964, pp. 398-401.
[37] Fig. 4 shows that most of the very populous dioceses in Mexico are "over-supplied" with ecclesiastical services, relative to the national median.
[38] Latourette, op. cit., Vol. 3, p. 164.

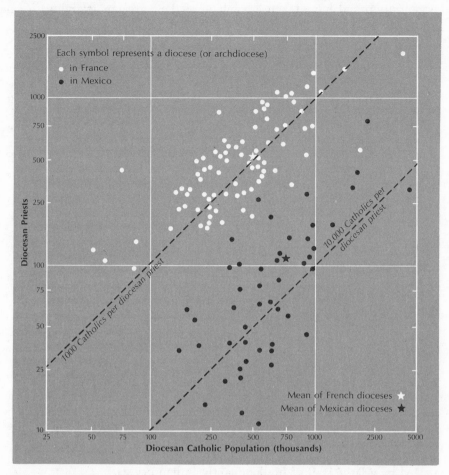

FIG. 4. *Ratio of diocesan (secular) priests to Catholic population in France and Mexico, ca. 1960. Scales are logarithmic. (Data from* Annuario Pontificio, *1963.)*

diocesan priest are to be found in such demographically stagnant, rural, and highly conservative areas as Brittany and the Cevennes in the southern Massif Central (Fig. 4).[39]

Urban society today presents the Church with organizational problems which the traditional structure was not designed to meet. The parish as a neighborhood with pedestrian circulation has become obsolete, especially in American cities. Moreover, there is a rising demand for a variety of church services. The financial organization of the Church remains parochial in such matters as religious schooling, and this parochial organization cannot perform satisfactorily. Protestant denominations in this country have been less bound by a traditional, fairly rigid

[39] Fig. 4 shows that most of the very populous dioceses in France are "undersupplied" with ecclesiastical services relative to the national median. In 1966, as an experimental countermeasure, the dioceses of Paris and Versailles were reorganized in seven dioceses; these are to cooperate through new institutional channels.

organization and have taken advantage of their greater flexibility to experiment with other ways of solving similar problems.

Regional variations in the spatial structure of the Catholic Church are nevertheless kept within limits. Over the centuries, some principles have been developed for the Catholic organization of space, especially in areas of growing Catholic population. New dioceses are formed as provisionally organized territory is brought into the hierarchy or when an existing diocese is divided to form two new ones. The appropriate papal authorities consider such geographical factors as: size and distribution of the Catholic population in the proposed diocese; existing religious facilities, such as the number of priests, churches, schools; financial resources, which formerly usually consisted of revenue from endowments of land; availability of an urban center; size; ease of communication within the territory.[40] For the past two centuries, political boundaries and cultural boundaries such as those of language have also been considered as a matter of principle in drawing diocesan boundaries. Most state boundaries in the United States are also diocesan boundaries, and some Catholic dioceses correspond to individual states.

Catholic dioceses now in existence, numbering almost 2,000, have a considerable range of area and Catholic population. Non-European dioceses are generally several times larger than European ones, but often have a much smaller Catholic population. Within Europe, Italy has, for historical reasons, a disproportionately large number of territorial dioceses, apart from many titular ones. The Italian diocese has an average area of only 400 square miles compared to an area of 3,000 square miles in Spain.[41] German-speaking Catholics are markedly underrepresented compared to Italians to the extent that a bishop may be said to speak for a diocesan population. But regional imbalance in episcopal representation is by no means the chief element in the Italianate character of the Roman Church. This comes primarily from the control by Italian clerics of responsible executive positions in the papal offices, in which they are supported by a large staff of predominantly Italian priests.

Anomalies such as these are mostly the result of historical inertia. Reorganizing dioceses when there has been economic and demographic standstill or decline in an area takes a long time. The amalgamation of existing dioceses is far more difficult than the creation of new ones and is less likely to be initiated locally. In areas of rapidly growing Catholic population, however, the spatial pattern of the hierarchy is constantly modified to provide effective spiritual service, as shown by the contemporary increase in the number of dioceses in such countries as the United States, where, in the period 1900-1965, the number of diocesan units rose from 90 to 139.[42] In the Indian subcontinent, there are now 79 diocesan units in place of the 30 found in 1900.

Within dioceses and ecclesiastical provinces, sees appear to be located without much concern for centrality within these potential service territories. In the United States, the ecclesiastical center is often located very

[40] See the article "Diocese" in *The Catholic Encyclopedia*, ed. Charles G. Hebermann *et al.* (New York: Robert Appleton Company, 1907-1912, fifteen volumes).

[41] Dioceses in France were reorganized during Napoleon's regime to correspond to the newly created *départements*, but except in the Provence, French dioceses, too, had been notably larger than Italian ones since the Middle Ages.

[42] In the conterminous 48 states.

close to a diocesan boundary. Even close urban neighbors provide the sees of different dioceses, as do Cincinnati, Ohio/Covington, Kentucky, and Kansas City, Kansas/Kansas City, Missouri. Chicago and Milwaukee, though not far apart, are both the seats of archbishops. This pattern reflects the territorial growth of the Catholic Church as a centralized organism, establishing successive points of entry, beyond which lay what subsequently became service hinterlands.

A territorial organization such as this requires an effective network of communication and transportation. The Catholic Church has continually had to contend with attenuation or disruption of communication and therefore of its control, permitting the development of ethnic or regional churches. This has sometimes led to territorial disintegration, as in the final schism between the Eastern and Western churches in the eleventh century and the separation of much of northern Europe from Rome in the sixteenth. The conditions under which the Reformation developed and spread include such geographic ones as distance of the affected areas from Rome and regional variation in the organizational strength of the Catholic Church. The ecclesiastical geography of medieval Europe showed such unevenness in organization as a division of Sardinia into 18 dioceses and of Ireland into 31, while the whole territory of England and Wales, with its very much larger population, consisted of only 21 dioceses. Preceding the Reformation, there appears to have been a relative weakening of ecclesiastical communication and territorial organization in northern Europe, their development having failed to keep pace with population growth during the Middle Ages.

Weak parochial organization in Latin America results in a weakening of the ideological and social currents which the Church seeks to generate. Both Catholic and Protestant spokesmen consider this infrequency of communication a major reason for the remarkable success of Protestant missionary efforts in Latin America since World War II. In thirty years, the Protestant population of Latin America has grown from less than half a million to nine million. Frequent neo-Christian prophetic movements in Brazilian frontier territories must also have been facilitated and encouraged by the great shortage of priests there.[43]

With improved communications, on the other hand, the Roman Catholic Church was able to recover or to integrate for the first time some of the Eastern churches. The so-called Uniate churches of Syria and Lebanon and the Romo-Christians of Kerala in southwestern India were absorbed into the Catholic system following the intensified contact between them and Rome in the age of European overseas expansion.

The ordinary hierarchy of Catholic dioceses and parishes and its staff of secular clergy are supplemented in two ways. A provisional form of territorial organization, the mission, extends the area coming under the purview of the Church. Secondly, there are a number of religious orders, the regular clergy,[44] who are partly or completely independent of the territorial hierarchy in their spatial organization, being directly subordinate to Rome in some cases. These may perform specialized religious

---

[43] G. Guariglia, *Prophetismus und Heilserwartungsbewegungen als völkerkundliches und religionsgeschichtliches Problem,* Wiener Beiträge zur Kulturgeschichte und Linguistik, XIII (Horn-Wien: Berger, 1959), p. 185.

[44] "Regular" because they follow a monastic rule (Latin: *regula*).

tasks, such as teaching. They have also performed the functions of the secular clergy in such weakly organized areas as Latin America. Both monastic and military-religious orders played a major role in the expansion, consolidation, and revitalization of Catholic Christianity in Europe. Subsequently in the Americas, the Augustinian, Dominican, and Franciscan orders, joined later by the Jesuits, carried out the greater part of the work of converting and instructing the native population in the new religion.

MISSION GEOGRAPHY. A geography of missionary operations, both Catholic and Protestant, is needed for a proper evaluation of Christianity's role as a carrier of Western culture to the non-Western world, especially since 1800. Unfortunately, a comprehensive mapping of the extent and intensity of Christian missionary activity does not exist.

Missionary activity is often directed along lines of advance and based on strong points that are quite distinct from those of commercial or military geography. This is precisely because religious missions, in their uncorrupted form, are seeking to make contact with undifferentiated human beings, rather than to control sources of commodities or strategic sites. Thus, while the Dutch commercial-political enterprise in the East Indies followed the routes of the maritime trade previously dominated by Muslims, the later Christian missionary endeavor diverged from these in order to penetrate pagan hinterlands not known to be economically attractive.

The fact that missionary efforts are centrally organized requires that contact be maintained with headquarters for supplies and instructions. Transportation routes must be opened and missionary bases established, as in California, where the Franciscans established a chain of coastal missions in the eighteenth century. This Christian missionary thrust was, however, not unrelated to Spain's strategic interests along the western coast of North America. Christianization, moreover, does have the effect of bringing isolated areas into the world economic network. After the industrial revolution, this was seen by European nations as a useful byproduct of missionary activity. David Livingstone returned from his Congo exploration, according to one story, to seek support for missionary work from Manchester textile interests with the argument that Christianization of the Africans would create a demand for clothing and thus open up a large new market for Lancashire cottons.[45]

A remarkable geographic consequence of Christian missionary activity is the irregular distribution of Protestants and Catholics, and also of Protestant denominations, among the non-Western populations being propagandized. During the past 150 years, Catholic missionaries have been predominant in lands under the colonial rule of France and Belgium, while Protestant missionaries have been dominant, although less exclusively so, in British and Dutch colonial territories. The two Christian systems appear to have been making roughly equal efforts in the missionary field in recent years, with altogether about 60,000 Western missionaries working abroad.

Regionalization of the mission lands by Protestant denominations is a result of tacit understanding or formal agreements regarding a division

[45] Deffontaines, *op. cit.*, p. 255.

of territories and spheres of influence (comity). In eastern Asia, for example, Baptist missions predominate in Burma, the Methodists were once the dominant Protestant body in China, while the Presbyterian Church is well established as the leading Protestant church in Korea and Taiwan.

SACRED LANGUAGES. An important element in the religious organization of space is the use of special languages and scripts as the media of communication. Sacred languages, used in the performance of ritual or for the transmittal of religious knowledge from one generation to another, can also be important integrating symbols. However, the so-called "dead" liturgical languages should not be underrated as useful means of communication among learned men of different tongues sharing the same religion.

The early spread of Christianity was facilitated by the use of a common spoken Greek (*koine*) as the lingua franca of the eastern part of the Roman Empire. Christianity's subsequent diffusion in the western half of the Empire profited from the currency of Latin there, while the use of Aramaic as an international commercial language in the Fertile Crescent and Mesopotamia was an advantage for the Nestorian Church. The division of the Christian Church into eastern and western blocks reflects a partial breakdown in the communication of points of view and of regional interests that was a concomitant of Christendom's division into Greek-using and Latin-using regions. By sanctifying Latin as the liturgical language, the Roman Catholic Church provided a common language for religious and administrative communication among the clergy in the polyglot post-Roman world, even after Latin was no longer the mother tongue of living peoples. Hebrew, before its recent revival, had a similar liturgical function among dispersed Jewish communities, although it had long been displaced as the mother tongue of almost all Jews. Pali and Sanskrit are other dead but sacred languages which have provided means of communication among specialists and vehicles for the transmittal of sacred knowledge.

The relationship of Arabic to Islam is especially intimate. As the language of the sacred literature and the vehicle of the Islamic civilization, Arabic was widely diffused. From the seventh century on, its prestige as the language of Islam enabled it to displace the various mother tongues of the new Muslim populations of the Middle East.[46] In the course of time, most of the remaining Christian and Jewish neighbors of these Arabicized Muslims also acquired Arabic as their own mother tongue. Beyond this much enlarged area of Arabic speech, Arabic provided a means of communication for Islamic scholars having different mother tongues, and its script came to be used for the writing of such languages as Persian, Malay, and Turkish. The use of Arabic as the medium of Islamic scholarship and as the common liturgical language, however poorly understood by the non-Arab mass, reinforces the sense of religious kinship existing among Muslims. The orthodox still successfully oppose Muslim publication of the Koran in translation, except in the form of a gloss accompanying the Arabic text.

[46] The change was most striking in the Nile Valley, where the earlier language had not been a related Semitic one.

The use of distinctive hallowed forms of writing by certain religious communities occasionally provides a powerful symbol of religious differentiation. The writing of the same or closely related languages in different scripts by different religious communities is an element of cultural diversity in the Indian subcontinent. In northern India, Muslims and Hindus write essentially the same language with the two quite different alphabetic systems which are used for writing their sacred scriptures. At present or until recently, Sikhs and Goan Christians in India, Jews in Central Europe, and Serbs and Croats in Yugoslavia have been communities whose religious separateness has been reinforced by the use of distinctive scripts for writing the spoken language. These scripts have helped to differentiate them from people speaking much the same language but belonging to other religions.

Religious Organization and Political Organization

The geographic shape of political organizations and of political fields of force is exerting increasing effect on the human characteristics of places. The relationships between religious systems and political organization thus constitute a significant area of inquiry in the geography of religions. What follows is a brief survey of these relationships.[47]

Theocracy. In a theocracy, religious organization provides the machinery of government and exerts preponderant political power. Theocracy has never prevailed widely, even among the ethnic religions of antiquity. Rulers and priests were usually separate, as they are in the living ethnic religions of Shinto and Hinduism.[48]

Universalizing religious systems have achieved theocratic forms of control within certain regions, a process which has usually had a pronounced ethnicizing effect on the system locally. Tibet provides an example. The monastic hierarchy, which evolved out of Mahayana Buddhism, governed the country for about four centuries, thereby fostering a virtually ethnic religious system, Lamaism. Ultimately, this did spread to Mongol tribes to the north.

The Mormon domination of the Utah Territory in the nineteenth century constituted a theocracy, associated with a temporarily ethnicizing religious system. The religious hierarchy was also the hierarchy of civil government, and Mormon religious law was the civil law until effectively superseded by the acceptance of federal jurisdiction on the question of polygamy. As Mormonism evolved, the theocratic form was seen as necessary for the intended regulation of social and economic life, and the Church of Latter-Day Saints still considers itself a theocracy.[49]

In South America, the Jesuit government of eastern Paraguay and the adjoining Paraná region, with its center at Asunción, was a theocracy extending over more than 100,000 square miles. Charged with converting the Indian population, the Jesuits established missions and maintained a benevolent but despotic rule, carefully regulating morals and organiz-

[47] For a useful general discussion of an important aspect of the theme, see S. N. Eisenstadt, "Religious Organizations and Political Process in Centralized Empires," *Journal of Asian Studies,* XXI (1962), 271-94.
[48] Judaism was at one time the organizing principle of an ethnic theocracy, in the Maccabean period.
[49] O'Dea, *The Mormons,* p. 166.

ing the economy to provide the inhabitants with greater material comfort than was usual among Indian populations in Spanish territories. The system collapsed with the expulsion of the Jesuits in 1767, prompted by official suspicion and the resentment of other colonists.

State or established religions. The religious organization sometimes provides the state with ritual services and a measure of spiritual validation and is in turn protected, maintained, and favored over other religions by the state. Spiritual validation or sanctification of the ruler has been a common arrangement in the past; in one form, the ruler was recognized as a god.

In diluted form, this type of spiritual validation survives as one element in the relationship between an established religion and the state, the church validating the state which in turn protects it. The Church of England, as the established church in that country, is no longer given direct financial support by the government but benefits from large endowments that originally were provided by the state. In return, it submits to a degree of control by the state. Similar arrangements exist in Denmark, Norway, and Sweden, where the Lutheran Church is the established church. In these countries there is complete freedom of religion, but in Spain and a few Latin American countries, where Roman Catholicism is the official religion, others are only tolerated in a limited way.

In Islam, the early state organization derived validity from the relationship of the ruler to the founder of the religion, Muhammad. The Caliph—the title signified that he was a successor to Muhammad—was more than a secular ruler: he was the defender of the faith. In the absence of an effective bureaucratic organization of the religious system itself, the Caliph was also the manager of religious institutions. However, he was in no sense equivalent to the Pope, since the interpretation of scriptures depended on a consensus of legal scholars. Even in recent times, the government in dominantly Muslim nations such as Turkey and Syria has continued to supervise certain religious institutions, notably the *waqf*, or charitable endowment.

Use of the power and prestige of governments to support religious systems has had far-reaching consequences for the geographic distribution of religions. No event of this kind has had greater geographical significance than the Emperor Theodosius' establishment of Christianity as the official religion of the Roman Empire in A.D. 395.

A ruler's conversion—an idiosyncratic religious decision—may speak for the people under him. This happens in the conversion of tribal societies and small states marginal to religious realms (see Chapter 5). The responsibility for religious decisions often allowed to rulers is indicated by the relative ease with which Henry VIII of England could break away from the Roman Catholic Church, despite little popular support, and establish his own ethnic church.

In the seventeenth century, many state religions were established by treaty following the wars between Catholics and Protestants. In Germany in 1555, the Peace of Augsburg had adopted the principle succinctly expressed in the formula: *cujus regio ejus religio;* the religion of the ruler was to be the religion of the territory ruled by him. The same doctrine was asserted again in the Treaty of Westphalia in 1648, following the ruinous Thirty Years' War. The application of the formula was partly responsible for the patchy distribution of dominantly Protestant and dominantly Catholic areas still visible in West Germany.

Proscribed and penalized religions. The state proscribes and penalizes religions usually because some other religion is the official one or because the proscribed religion is seen as a political threat. The expulsion of Jews and Muslims from Spain following completion of the Christian reconquest in 1492 is one of numerous cases. The discriminatory Islamic poll tax (*jizya*) formerly levied on Christians, Jews, and Hindus, is another. Today various religions are officially penalized in a number of countries. Jews are excluded from Saudi Arabia. Christian missionaries have been expelled from Communist China and the Sudan. In several Communist countries, Christian churches operate under severe handicaps. Protestant missionary activity and even practice are curtailed in Spain and a few Latin American countries. For most of the period of Spanish rule, all non-Catholic foreigners were rigorously excluded from Spain's American possessions. Subsequently, some of the independent Latin American states forcefully discouraged Protestant missionary activity. Colombia and Peru are still charged with supporting discrimination against non-Catholics.[50]

The secular state. With the growth of secularism, many modern governments are predicated on the separation of church and state, aiming ostensibly at elimination of special government recognition of any religion. The absolute realization of the ideal is hardly to be expected, but a limited expression of it does create opportunities for religious diversification and competitive coexistence among different religious systems. Thus, the relatively late separation of church and state in some Latin American countries could be exploited by Protestantism, whose vigorous missionary activities have since had great success.

Religious communities as nations. Some religious systems have created religious communities which have formed the basis of new nations or national minorities. Followers of the same religion, feeling a common identity, may also share certain culture traits that differentiate them from other religious communities in the same region. Incompatible ideological elements may occur in two such religious subcultures, leading the two communities to become socially separate. Conflicting interests and a traditional antagonism may develop. A new nation or national minority can come into being under such circumstances, especially when the religious subcultures predominate in certain territories.

In the formation of new nationalities, religious differences sometimes reinforce the primary role played by language. Thus, the current ethnic conflict in Ceylon is primarily between the majority Sinhalese-speaking population and the minority Tamil-speaking one. These communities are predominantly Buddhist and predominantly Hindu, respectively, a difference that appears to be of secondary political importance.

However, a particular religious identity can by itself become the basis of a movement for separate national identity. The separation of Belgium, comprising two markedly different linguistic communities, from the Netherlands in the 1830's was motivated by the desire of a predominantly

[50] H. Wakelin Coxill and Kenneth Grubb, eds., *World Christian Handbook,* 1962 (London: World Dominion Press, 1962), pp. 47-48.

Catholic population in a compact territory, Belgium, to be politically separate from a chiefly Calvinist one.

An ancient ethnic population, the Irish, is today split because of religious differences into two nationally distinct groups, the predominantly Catholic people of independent Eire and a population having a Presbyterian core in Northern Ireland, part of the United Kingdom. The attempt of the Irish of Eire to find a common linguistic basis for unity of the whole island is futile, since the existence of an independent Ireland is almost entirely based on the historic circumstance of religious differentiation, the common language of Eire, Northern Ireland, and the rest of the British Isles being English.

In the pre-Reformation period "Irish" had meant "Gaelic." After the Reformation "Irish" gradually became identified with "Roman Catholic" when the Gaels (the "Old Irish") and the Old English and Scots (or "New Irish") were welded together as "Papists" by discrimination and suppression on a politicoreligious basis. Thus was formed the modern "Irish nation" . . . Irish nationalism has nearly always expressed itself in the English language.[51]

In less violent fashion, the ethnicism of the Scots and Welsh has become detached from linguistic differentiation and attached to and integrated by a "national" Protestant religious system, the Presbyterian Church of Scotland and the Welsh Methodist Church, respectively. In Wales, the establishment of Methodism in the eighteenth century utilized the Welsh translation of the Bible and in becoming virtually a national church helped Welsh to hold its ground as the language of the home far more successfully than Irish (Gaelic) did in Ireland.[52]

Overt claims to independent nationhood on the part of religious communities have recently led to the creation of two nations, Pakistan and Israel. Both consider themselves to be states that provide political and territorial expression for a religious community. Pakistan calls itself an Islamic state. Both have had as a result a sense of obligation to maintain religious institutions and traditions. In Israel, for example, all persons identified as Jews are subject to religious law in matters of marriage and divorce. Ireland is, in the same sense, a Catholic state, in that Catholic teaching on social problems was embodied in the constitution at the time of its creation.

Religion and political parties. In many contemporary secular states, religious organizations and religious communities form the basis of political parties. In addition to parties representing national religious minorities, there are parties which represent the social and economic viewpoints of religious communities or the active membership of a group of churches. Parties like this, such as the Christian Democratic Party in West Germany, are not uncommon in Europe.[53]

More directly concerned with specifically religious issues are parties with vague political aims, other than their demand for laws embodying orthodox religious requirements and restrictions. The Hindu Mahasabha

---

[51] Heslinga, *op. cit.*, p. 203.

[52] J. Wreford Watson and J. A. Sissons, *The British Isles: a Systematic Geography* (London: Thomas Nelson & Sons, 1964), pp. 404, 413.

[53] Eric Fischer, "Religions: Their Distribution and Role in Political Geography," in *Principles of Political Geography,* ed. Hans W. Weigert *et al.* (New York: Appleton-Century-Crofts, 1957), pp. 434-38.

in India and the Mizrahi party in Israel are minority parties which represent a sectarian orthodoxy in the religion of the majority. Their point of view has not been overtly challenged in those countries because the religious identity of the majority is in both cases closely tied to the concept of the nation itself.

Religious organizations which are also political organizations are less common; a number of new Asian sects and segmental religions are of this type. In South Vietnam, the hierarchical organization of the syncretic religion called Cao Dai, which is estimated to have a following of two million, is simultaneously a political organization. The Japanese Buddhist sect called Soka Gakkai is currently expanding very rapidly as a political party with a nationalistic platform.

Political expression of religious realms. The whole area dominated by a major religious system rarely has political unity. It is true that both Christianity and Islam, as universalizing systems, aspired first to create community-nations which would preserve their religious message and transmit it to the rest of mankind. The New Testament speaks of the Christian community as forming "an holy nation, a peculiar people . . . which in time past were not a people, but are now the people of God." [54] But in a political sense these aspirations were never fulfilled.

After the Roman Empire disintegrated, a form of partial Christian political unity remained within the Roman Catholic realm. The temporal powers being weak or in disorder, the Church, through its hierarchical organization of space, could exercise political control over the regions under its spiritual authority. Between the end of the eleventh century and the beginning of the thirteenth, the Catholic Christian world, especially the part to the north of the Mediterranean lands, participated in a joint military effort seeking to displace Islam from control of the Holy Land. After that, the possibility of a unified political organization of the Catholic lands of Europe faded, to be utterly dissipated by the Reformation.

Nevertheless, the idea of a Christian realm, opposed in an alternately hot and cold war to the Muslim realm (Fig. 5), appears to have been a critical element in the development of the concept of Europe as a cultural realm and of Europeans as a culture group. On the Muslim-dominated coasts of the Near East and southern Asia, Europeans of all nationalities were still known in the sixteenth century by the group name of *Faranji* or *Feringhi*, meaning "the Franks," the same name that had been used to denote the mixed ethnos of the Crusaders three hundred years earlier. The nineteenth century association of "Christian Powers" in the Concert of Europe was a late echo of the idea of Europe as Christendom, revived briefly by the confrontation with Muslim Turkey. The political force of their common identity as Christian nations was, however, practically nil.

By the nineteenth century and indeed long before that, early Islam's political unity had also disintegrated, and the possibility of concerted political action of any kind by the Muslim world had become quite remote. [55] Locally, Islam has had some success as a political cement. Indeed,

[54] I Peter 2:9-10.
[55] In the sixteenth century, a coalition of Muslim powers made an abortive attempt to eject the intruding Portuguese from the Indian Ocean, which previously had been virtually an Islamic sea. It was the last significant action of the kind.

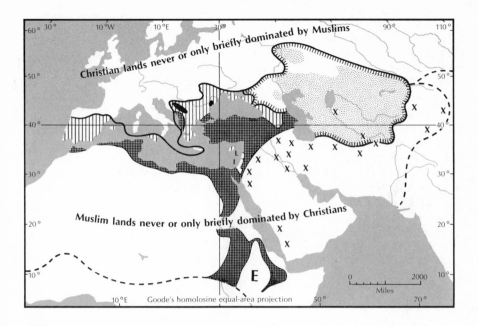

Once dominantly Christian, conquered by Muslims; Muslims now numerically dominant.

Once dominantly Christian, conquered and ruled by Muslims for more than 200 years, reconquered by Christians; Christians now numerically dominant.

Within the preceding category, Muslims locally dominant or a large minority.

Previously non-Christian lands dominantly Muslim for more than 200 years, presently under Christian rule.

Within the preceding category, Muslims locally dominant or a large minority.

E   Ethiopia: Christian, never dominated by Muslims.

I   Israel: much contested by Christians and Muslims; neither dominant at present.

L   Lebanon: much contested by Christians and Muslims; Christian/Muslim equilibrium at present.

X   Areas of Nestorian Christian strength, overrun and reduced by Muslims.

FIG. 5.   *The Christian/Muslim front in Europe and the Middle East, seventh to twentieth centuries.*

the linking of the dissimilar and even antipathetic East and West Pakistan to form a single nation might be regarded as one of its triumphs. Islam also helps to integrate mutually hostile linguistic groups in the new nation-states of Algeria and Morocco.

On a broader scale, the Pan-Islamic movements of the early part of this century had little success, perhaps because, as Toynbee thinks, Islam as a religious system was never seriously threatened.[56] The growth of nationalism in most of the Muslim world since then makes the success of such Pan-Islamic programs seem even less likely now.

In one sense, Islam has succeeded in creating a nation that is still seeking its appropriate political expression. This is not the 'umma, or Islamic world community, but the Arabic-speaking portion of it, the "Arab nation" created by the spread of the religion and its sacred language in a region of previous ethnic diversity and of ethnicized Christian churches. Only recently has a consciousness of Arab nationhood begun to grow, and only in this generation has this Arab nationalism begun to draw some of the remnant Christian Arabs into its fold.

[56] Toynbee, *Study of History,* Vol. 8, 692ff.

CHAPTER 5   *the distribution*
of religions

Only a few religious systems together command the adherence of more than three-quarters of mankind. Each of these major systems is predominant over large areas which constitute religious realms (Fig. 6). Here, the distributions discussed include people with nominal adherence, as well as areas where the religious tradition has recently been overlaid by Communism.

The largest and most populous religious realm is the Christian one, extending over Europe, the Americas, much of northern Asia, South Africa, Australia, and Oceania, excluding certain sparsely populated interior lands outside Europe. Christendom is divided into almost completely separate realms, over most of which a major Christian subsystem predominates. Of these the Roman Catholic realm is the largest. In Europe, there is often a sharp boundary between areas where Roman Catholics make up at least 90 per cent of the population and areas where they are in a minority of 10 per cent or less. Exceptions occur in Central Europe, where areas of Catholic numerical predominance and insignificance occur in a fragmented pattern together with areas where Catholics and Protestants are in closer balance. Catholics comprise 45 per cent of the population of Switzerland and 40 per cent of the population of the Netherlands, but both countries are divided into strongly Catholic and strongly Protestant areas. The predominantly Catholic lands of Europe are Ireland, France, Belgium, Spain, Portugal, Italy, Austria, the Slovenian, Croatian, and Dalmatian provinces of Yugoslavia, the Czech territory, Poland—now including the area along the Baltic recently vacated by German Lutherans—and Lithuania. In addition there are blocks of Catholic dominance in the southern Netherlands, West Germany, especially in Bavaria and the land bounded by the Rhine and Moselle, central and southern Switzerland, and the Hungarian, Slovak, and Rumanian lands.

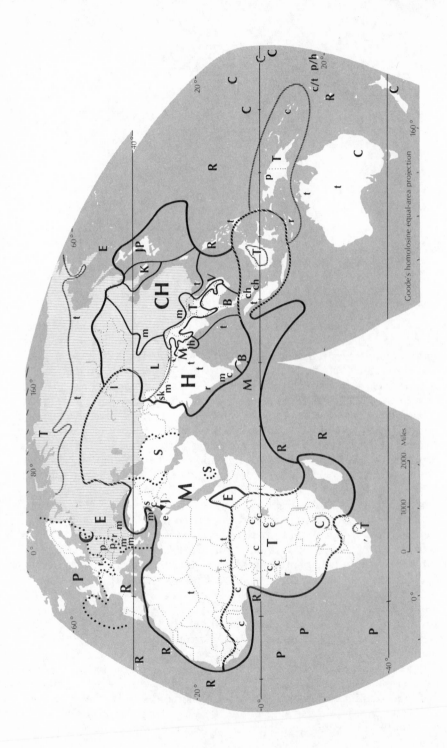

Goode's homolosine equal-area projection

c/t p/h

2000 Miles

1000

0

Size of letters indicates importance;
for example:

C   Major religious realm

C   Dominant religion

c   Minority religion, in places locally dominant

Major religious boundary

Minor religious boundary

Major transition zone

Minor transition zone

Boundary within major religious system

Countries under Communist regimes

B   Theravada Buddhism

C   Undifferentiated Christianity

CH   Chinese ethnic complex

E   Eastern Orthodox Christianity

H   Hinduism

JP   Japanese ethnic complex

J   Judaism

K   Korean ethnic complex

L   Lamaism

M   Islam, predominantly Sunni

P   Protestantism, including Anglican Church

R   Roman Catholicism

S   Shia Islam

SK   Sikhism

T   Tribal or simple ethnic religions

V   Vietnamese ethnic complex

FIG. 6. *Distribution of religions in the Old World.*

Great Britain and a core area in Northern Ireland, the northern Netherlands, Scandinavia, Finland, Estonia, most of the North German Plain, and Central Germany east of the Weser are predominantly Protestant.[1] To the east and southeast of the Protestant and Catholic realms in Europe, the Eastern Orthodox Churches have had dominance. Some Orthodox communities on the margin of the Catholic realm, in Galicia and northern Rumania, have been affiliated with Rome as Uniate churches, but they have broken away recently under political pressure. The major Christian systems are fragmented and interspersed in and around the Carpathian mountain block. Catholic, Protestant, Greek Orthodox, and Greek Uniate communities are found here, including a large Calvinist Protestant minority in the eastern plain of Hungary east of the Tiszta River. Within Europe, Muslim majorities occur in most of Albania, some districts in Bosnia and southern Serbia, the Dobruja between the lower Danube and the Black Sea, and Turkey-in-Europe. Eastward, the tradition of the Russian Orthodox Church is predominant in Russian-speaking lands and in most of the Caucasus.

Catholicism is predominant in Latin America, except for areas of unconverted simple societies and countries in the Guianas and the Caribbean that have been influenced by British and Dutch rule. Within Anglo-America, Catholicism is predominant in French-speaking Quebec. There are other small areas of Catholic dominance, including some northeastern cities, but most of the United States and Canada have a Catholic minority comprising about 15 to 35 per cent of the population (Fig. 7).[2] The exceptions, where Catholics are in a very small minority, are the Mormon country and the South—excluding southern Louisiana and parts of Florida and Texas—which is dominated by Baptist churches (Fig. 8). South Africa is predominantly Protestant, but the English-speaking Christian areas of Australia and Oceania have considerable Catholic minorities. Two isolated regions of Christian dominance are found in the Old World: the dominantly Catholic lands in the Philippine Islands and the Amharic core of Ethiopia with its virtually autonomous church.

The remaining religious realms occupy most of Asia and Africa. The Islamic realm, Dar al-Islam, is the most extensive in area, but has fewer followers than the Chinese religious system, and only slightly more than Hinduism. Across North Africa and the Middle East to Afghanistan and West Pakistan stretches a contiguous territory in which Muslims predominate, except for the Jewish and Christian toeholds on the Levantine coast. Western Syria and Lebanon, where Christianity and Islam have interacted vigorously since the seventh century, have considerable religious diversity. The Sunni Muslim majority comprises about 55 per cent of the population, while all Muslims, including Druzes, constitute only three-quarters of the region's population. In East Pakistan, the Soviet province of Kazakhstan, Malaya, and some of the outer islands of Indonesia, Muslims also have moderate to heavy majorities. The island of

[1] Including Anglicans, dominant only in England.
[2] For detailed religious distributions in the United States, including distributions of many Protestant denominations, see W. Zelinsky, "An Approach to the Religious Geography of the United States," *Annals*, Association of American Geographers, LI (1961), 139-93. Maps showing the distribution of Roman Catholics are on pp. 168-70.

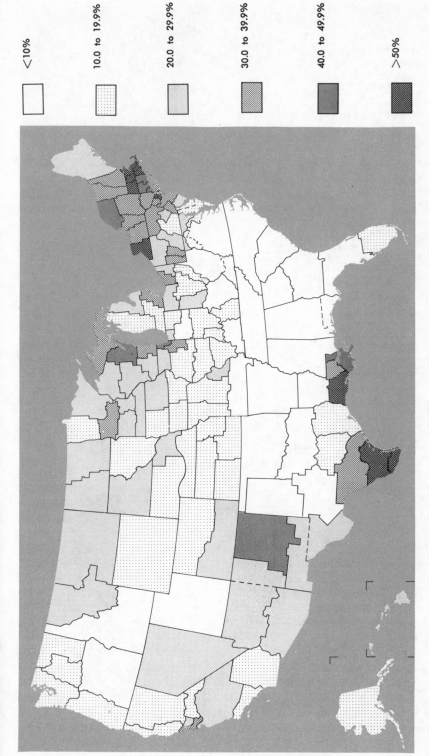

FIG. 7. *Roman Catholics in total U.S. population, ca. 1960. Data by dioceses. Broken lines represent state boundaries within dioceses. (Sources: World Catholic Almanac, 1964; Map of the Archdioceses and Dioceses of the United States. Washington, D.C.: National Catholic Welfare Conference, 1965.)*

<10%

10.0 to 19.9%

20.0 to 29.9%

30.0 to 39.9%

40.0 to 49.9%

>50%

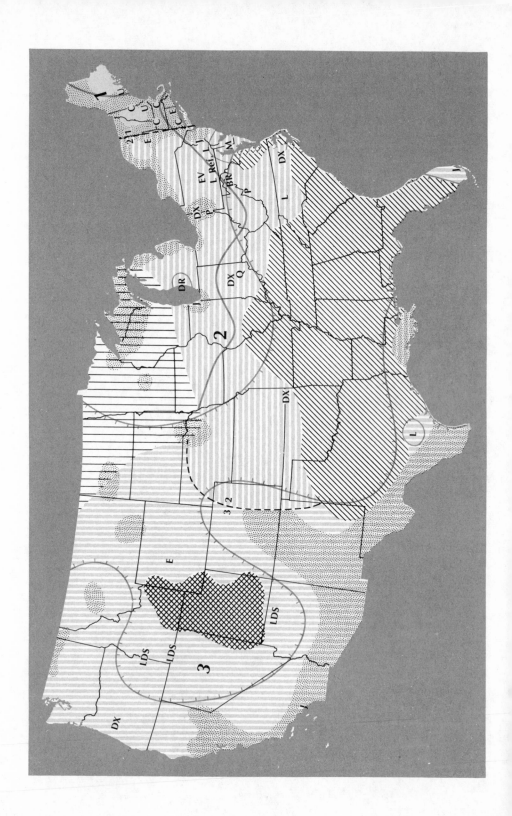

Moderate to high Protestant diversity; Baptists, Lutherans, Methodists, and Presbyterians not distinguished separately.

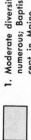

1. Moderate diversity: Lutherans not numerous; Baptists a minority except in Maine.

2. Fairly high Protestant diversity: Methodists generally the leading denomination.

3. Very high Protestant diversity.

Moderately low Protestant diversity: Lutherans dominant.

Low religious diversity: Baptists and Methodists together predominant; Catholics not numerous.

Very low religious diversity: Mormons predominant.

Catholics locally dominant or a large minority; separate urban concentrations not shown.

Area within which Catholics and Jews together comprise less than 25 per cent of city populations.

Southern limit of region (east of Missouri River) where Baptists are rarely the leading Protestant denomination.

Numerically significant minority denominations, sometimes most numerous locally (other than Baptists, Methodists, Lutherans, Presbyterians, and Roman Catholics).

BR Brethren

C Congregational

DR Dutch Reformed

DX Disciples of Christ

E Episcopalian

EV Evangelical

J Jewish

L Lutheran

LDS Mormon

M Methodist

P Presbyterian

Q Quaker (Friends)

Ref Reformed

U Unitarian-Universalist

 Locally dominant.

FIG. 8. *Religious affiliation in the United States, ca. 1950.*

Java, with approximately one-seventh of the world's Muslims, is again marked by Muslim predominance. Within Dar al-Islam, the sedentary population of Iran with some of the rural people of southern Iraq comprise a distinct Shiite province.

The Buddhist realm consists of two separate blocks. Theravada Buddhism straddles the Bay of Bengal and occupies most of Ceylon, Burma, Thailand, Laos, and Cambodia, while the Lamaistic form of Mahayana Buddhism, now largely eradicated, has been the dominant system in Tibet, parts of Sinkiang, and Mongolia. Elsewhere in southern and eastern Asia, the Oriental ethnic religious systems are dominant.

Simple tribal religions occupy large areas in the humid tropics and in the boreal forests and tundra lands of North America and the Soviet Union. The populations involved are usually sparse, but locally in West Africa and southeastern Africa—in Malawi, Zambia, and Mozambique—there are considerable concentrations of people who adhere to one or another of the many simple ethnic religions of the region, each of which occupies only a small territory.

A discontinuous distribution, usually as minority communities, of adherents of a religion that typically lacks a core area of dominance is a diaspora, a word used originally for the distribution of Jews. Other diasporas are the Zoroastrian, chiefly represented by the Parsis of India, and the Armenian Christian. The term is sometimes used of a scattered distribution outside an extant core of dominance, as in speaking of a modern Hindu diaspora in East Africa, Southeast Asia, the West Indies, and elsewhere.

Processes of Spatial Growth

Religious distributions are generated by such processes of spatial interaction as diffusion, migration, and competition for space. Significantly affecting these processes are the relative ethnicity or universality of religious concepts, the simplicity or complexity of ritual, and the flexibility or rigidity of organization.

The diffusion of religions is particularly important to cultural geography because religious conversion is a key to the transmittal of a broad range of culture goods. Major ethnic and universalizing religions have had an important role as civilizing agencies among politically unorganized tribal groups and petty states. For such peoples, the simple act of conversion to one of the universalizing religions can be very much like throwing a switch: it permits an immediate inflow of ideas and cultural goods which were previously shut out as alien or incompatible with the existing system of belief.

MIGRATION. One obvious way cultural institutions grow is by the natural increase of the people who carry the culture. Differences in religious principles and social institutions result in differences in the demographic rates of religious communities. Territorial expansion results from population growth if this is accompanied by some movement of people.

The migration of simple ethnic religious systems usually results within a short time in the formation of new ones. Polynesian religion comprises the common religious elements spread by Polynesian migrations in the

Pacific Ocean, but these did not, except perhaps briefly, disperse a religious system creating a common identity among its adherents. The very nature of compound or complex ethnic systems leads to a certain amount of drag on mobility. The major ethnic religious realms have for the most part grown slowly, partly by short-distance migration of frontiersmen and partly by the often concomitant absorption of neighboring population through contact conversion.

Diasporas are a special case of the migration of ethnic religious systems. Selective, relatively long-range movements, in response to special combinations of "push" and "pull," are involved, as illustrated by the Jewish Diaspora.

The "exile" of Jewish communities in the Mediterranean world and its desert fringe was in part self-imposed. Jewish artisans and merchants, attracted by the commercial opportunities created by the Pax Romana, were already going abroad before the Roman destruction of the Jewish state. Similar opportunities subsequently led to the establishment of Jewish communities elsewhere in Asia. In Muslim countries, their identity was often maintained, but became blurred in non-Muslim Asia. Jewish communities in Christian Europe, distinguished by their role in the evolution of Christianity, underwent repeated persecution and displacement by force. They were expelled from England in 1290 not to return until the seventeenth century. Like the Muslims, they were expelled from Spain and Portugal at the end of the fifteenth century; it is estimated that between 200,000 and 400,000 were displaced. Subsequently both Jews and Muslims, including second and third generation converts to Christianity, were barred from migrating to Iberian territories in the Indies.

A combination of economic opportunity in eastern Europe during the Middle Ages, as German urbanizing influences spread eastward, together with the push of increasing animosity in the west accompanying the religious revival within the Catholic Church, gave rise to a plural society on the eastern front of Catholic Christendom. Jewish artisans, shopkeepers, and traders formed large minority blocks in the cities and in the smallest country towns.

In Poland, Lithuania, and the western border provinces of the Russian Empire, the largest block of Jewish population anywhere in the world had come into being by the beginning of this century. From this region, two major shifts of population occurred. One was the wave of migration to the United States, focusing on the northeastern cities; the New York metropolitan area now contains about a quarter of the world's Jews. The other was a flow of settlers to Palestine, where Jews of eastern European stock form the numerically and socially dominant stratum in the mixed Jewish population of Israel. In eastern Europe itself, Polish and Russian pogroms and later the policy of extermination executed by Nazi Germany all but wiped out the Jewish population. Farther east, however, about two million persons of Jewish descent are still living in Russia and other parts of the Soviet Union.

The scattered nucleations of Jewish population in the Diaspora are a product of continual selective migration of Jews to towns and cities. Other religious communities have sought other destinations when forced to migrate. In the Middle East, relatively inaccessible or unattractive mountain and desert lands have provided areas of refuge. Maronite

Christians, Alawi and Ismaili Muslim sects, Druzes, Yezidis and seces-sionist Muslim Kharijites have preserved their separate identities by accepting a degree of isolation. Other persecuted religious communities, such as the Mennonites, have sought a favorable reception in areas of agricultural opportunity in order to preserve their particular social values, the Mennonite search leading them as far afield as Kansas, Paraguay, and the Volga.

In other migrations, religious systems have extended their territories as the migrants became dominant in numbers in new lands. Buddhism and Islam have not grown much by this process, which has accounted for so much of Christianity's expansion in recent centuries. The Buddhist and Muslim communities that migrated *en masse* to new lands were mo-bile pastoral nomads, who, after conversion to the universalizing religion, preempted some part of the dry lands of Asia or northern Africa. The migration of Seljuk Turks as new converts to Islam into the semiarid, sparsely populated Anatolian Basin during the tenth and eleventh cen-turies was one consequential event of this kind. Most of Anatolia sub-sequently became Muslim by contact conversion of the Christian urban and peasant population.

Christian population migrations have made dramatic changes on the map of world religions.[3] European expansion has enlarged the Christian realm to many times what it was in 1500. Small numbers of immigrant Christians have sometimes created new Christian communities out of the indigenous population by conversion, and in part by intermarriage, as happened in much of Latin America. During the past two centuries, however, the migration and settlement of Christian populations has been the chief process producing new religious distributions. Mainly in this way, Christianity has become dominant in almost all of North America, Brazil, and extratropical South America, Australia, and New Zealand, in the South African areas settled by the Boers, and in the Siberian and Far Eastern lands settled by Russians of the Orthodox Church.

In the United States, the distribution of Christian communities is com-plex, with about 225 Protestant denominations and sects presently active. This diversity is partly a result of separate migrations of Europeans with their ethnicized churches, both established and dissident. The ethnic diversity of the Catholic population is, by contrast, concealed in the distribution of a uniform Catholicism.

Some major Christian communities in the United States have not been affected much by evangelization or contact conversion other than through intermarriage, and therefore have distributions that are largely the result of internal migration. The Catholic Church, the Lutheran churches, and the Orthodox churches remain ethnically distinct, most of their adherents in the United States being descendants of non-English immigrants. So are a number of sects, like the Amish. The distribution of many native American denominations also results from internal migra-tions, the occupance of Utah and adjacent states by the immigration of Mormons from the east being analogous to the Christian occupance of North America.

[3] See, e.g., the map entitled "Europeanization of the World," in Wilbur Zelinsky, *A Prologue to Population Geography* (Englewood Cliffs, N.J.: Prentice-Hall, Inc., 1966), pp. 74-75.

The Catholic population in the United States has grown spectacularly by migration in the past 125 years. With the exception of old Catholic populations in the territories acquired from France and Mexico and English Catholics in colonial Maryland, the great bulk of the Catholic population of the United States comes from mass migrations into the urban-industrial northeast that began in the 1840's and brought Irish, Germans, Poles, Italians, and most recently Puerto Ricans into the country. In 1840, the Catholic population of the United States was 663,000, less than 4 per cent of the total. It is now approximately 45 million, almost a quarter of the country's population.

CONTACT CONVERSION. Religious systems also grow by contact conversion. This often follows close interaction between two groups, especially when the convert group is technologically more backward than the other. The contact of the Indian and the Chinese civilizations with peripheral tribal folk who were then enveloped by the expanding civilization has, over the centuries, brought about a progressive acculturation of the tribal societies. In many cases, these have been absorbed into the body social of the dominant civilization, whose complex ethnic religious system replaces the tribal religion. Prestige, economic advantage, and security within a stable political order are inducements which the elaborate ethnic religious system offers the adherents of simple tribal religions. Even an ethnic religious system as complex in its ritual and as self-isolating in its relations with other communities as that of the Jews has acquired new members by contact conversion. Household servants and other economically dependent clients are a common source of converts.

Intermarriage that brings an alien spouse into the cultural and religious life of a community is often an important part of contact conversion. Information on such matters is scarce, but it would seem from demographic, anthropometric, and genetic data that marriage by outsiders into Jewish communities has not been uncommon. It is likely, too, that marriage out of the Jewish community into the surrounding Christian or Muslim communities has been even more frequent. Today the trend in this direction, a consequence of the decay of traditional religious systems, is very strong in the United States and has been retarded in Israel only by strict legal measures.

The role of intermarriage among people of different religions tells something about the relationships among the religious systems themselves. In one sense, universalizing systems exhibit an ethnicizing tendency when they prevent a believer from marrying a nonbeliever; in the long run, this prohibition creates a new breeding population, that is, an ethnic community.

The universalizing religious systems also grow by contact conversion, although often they owe more to missionary activity. In Islam, however, formal missionary organizations have not been common; rather, those who profess the faith seek individually to spread it by example and persuasion. Islam has acquired large areas of dense population by contact conversion supplemented by the missionizing efforts of lay persons. Islam spread by sea to the lands bordering the Indian Ocean in this way. Small numbers of Muslim mercantile folk settled and intermarried at ports of trade on the coasts of non-Muslim lands, in time extending their spheres of commercial interest and concomitantly the range of Islam into the hinterland. New converts to Islam among their clients and trading associates acquired elements of the polity and economy of Islam as presented in the canon law and, thus enrolled in an organized international community, in turn operated as agents of contact conversion in more distant areas. Most Muslims in coastal Indonesia, Malaya, and the southern Philippines as well as the smaller groups in southern India, Ceylon, and the Maldive Islands are products of this process. The same process has been important along the caravan trade routes of the northern dry lands, especially in Central Asia and the Sudan.

Various economic and cultural factors affect the success of contact conversion. A religious system acquires prestige by becoming the religion of the ruler or ruling class and thereby spreads rapidly. Among simple tribal societies it may suffice for the chief to be converted for the decision to have effect for the whole tribe. There were, for example, occasional mass conversions of American Indians by Spanish clergy, in which baptism of the leaders served vicariously to give thousands of their followers ritual admission into the Christian world.

The prestige of Muslim rulers, either conquerors or converts following conquest, has certainly helped Islam to spread. The gains which Islam could expect to make by conversion of subject populations were the goal of the *jihād*, or holy war. More or less voluntary conversion of Christians took place after the Arabs and Berbers conquered most of the Iberian Peninsula in the eighth century. Although Muslims remained in the minority, in Andalusia in the tenth and eleventh centuries, Muslims descended from Spanish Christians outnumbered those of Arab and Berber origin.[4] Transference of religious allegiance quickly followed the Muslim conquest of Persia, where the prevailing Zoroastrianism had had little popular appeal. Bengal and Kashmir are the two previously Hindu territories which appear to have experienced the swiftest mass conversion of much of the population following conquest by Muslim armies. In both these Indian areas, however, most of the competing elite of Brahmans and other highly placed castes did not follow the masses into the new religion.

In what is now the Arab Middle East, the conversion of the earlier Christian, Jewish, Zoroastrian, and Manichaean population proceeded more slowly, with perhaps only a tenth of the population belonging to Islam 150 years after its birth. As the Islamic civilization established itself, voluntary conversion increased. By 1250, most of the population was Muslim. Another large Muslim population, the Javanese, could not have been brought into the Islamic community had not the critical step of swaying the Javanese elite been taken, thus opening the way to conversion of the rural population.

In the United States, social and cultural factors are thought to influence denominational adherence in a significant way. The Episcopal Church, whose membership ranks high on various scales measuring social position,[5] has experienced a comparatively rapid rise in membership in the prosperous postwar decades, especially in the expanding high- and

[4] Toynbee, *Study of History*, Vol. 8, pp. 366n., 727.
[5] Bernard Lazerwitz, "A Comparison of Major United States Religious Groups," *Journal of the American Statistical Association*, LVI (1961), 568-79.

middle-income suburbs. This has been in part attributed to the social prestige of the Church.

A prime attraction of universalizing religions is that they afford membership in a world order, while at the same time providing a comprehensive explanation of the universe and man's place in it.[6] It is precisely when the constricted identity provided by a simple tribal religion becomes untenable because of changed spatial relationships that the universalizing system becomes most attractive. People on the periphery of a universalizing religious system have on occasion reached out to join it in order to acquire a satisfying identity. The process is a familiar one where the peripheral group is a tribal society. It can also occur within a complexly organized society, as it does today among particular groups in India and the United States. In Hindu India, the socially dispossessed strata in the western Indian state of Maharashtra have been seeking a more respectable status than that of Hindu untouchables while shunning affiliation with Islam or Christianity. Instead, they have found a solution in the adoption of Buddhism, which has had virtually no presence in Maharashtra for many centuries. In the United States, some American Negroes have been seeking through the Black Muslim movement to assume the identity conferred by the Old World religious system of Islam. Islam is seen by the followers of the ethnicizing segmental Black Muslim religion as being more favorable toward the Negro than American Christianity, which is regarded as having an unattractive (White) ethnic personality.

Contact conversion may be stimulated by the anticipation of economic advantages: financial assistance, education, or special employment or business opportunities. The pejorative term "rice Christians" is used of people in the Orient who are thought to have adopted Christianity for the material advantages of being Christian in areas under European dominance. Under Islamic governments, avoidance of the *jizya,* or poll tax, may have provided some people with an economic inducement to become Muslims.

ORGANIZED MISSIONS. Universalizing systems have developed different institutional machinery in accordance with their own forms of organization to implement their sense of mission. In Buddhism, the basic institutional person is the *bhikshu,* or monk, a member of a specialized religious community who teaches the principles of the religion to laymen. Organizations of monks have thus been the means of maintaining the religion and the chief agency in its spread. The Christian church system requires a secular clergy for its maintenance. These are primarily ritualists and spiritual caretakers serving fixed communities, so that missionary aspirations have had to be realized through specialized secondary agencies. Islam, with no hierarchical organization of specialists at all, has been correspondingly defective in specifically missionary organizations. These different ways of realizing missionary goals have affected the way each religion has spread.

Buddhist missionizing activity, directed toward the establishment of

6 Cf. Wilbert E. Moore, *Social Change* (Englewood Cliffs, N.J.: Prentice-Hall, Inc., 1963), p. 87.

monastic associations and their support by lay communities, was taken out of its North Indian context and given international scope by the Buddhist Emperor Asoka. Particularly in its Theravada form, Buddhism does not insist on a pronounced commitment from the society that supports it. In India and China, although widespread and with support in high places, it remained a minority religion. Without a highly centralized, hierarchical organization, it experienced difficulty in penetrating resistant areas and consolidating new territories.

In India, this virtually stratal religion was displaced by the reinvigorated popular institutions of Brahmanic Hinduism. Buddhism has had its most lasting success as a popular religion in Ceylon, Burma, and Thailand, which were relatively underdeveloped when Buddhist missions appeared there as culture-bearers of the high civilization of India. Mahayana Buddhism may have had greater success in Japan than it did in China because it appeared in Japan as a bearer of the more advanced T'ang civilization of China. However, the Buddhist advance into purely tribal country, such as much of highland Southeast Asia, has been relatively slow. This may be because the system has to depend for its support on a more complex form of political and economic organization than is found in tribal society.

Manichaeism was probably influenced by Buddhism and, like it, had a specialized celibate community, which could circulate as a powerful instrument for the propagation of the religion.

Organization for the purpose of implementing the missionary ideal in Islam is weakly developed. As with other Islamic institutions, propagation of the faith is tied to political organization. From Islam's beginnings, opportunity for growth has been foreseen from the extension of Muslim power. This policy has been wrongly interpreted as an attempt to win conversion "by the sword," implying a choice between conversion or death. In fact, conversion by the threat of death or violence has been rarer in Islam than in Christianity and is specifically forbidden in the Koran.[7]

The spread of Islam in conquered lands often proceeded slowly at first. Missionary activity has usually consisted of unorganized individual efforts, sometimes associated with movements of popular religious enthusiasm. Muslim historians ascribe Islam's success in eastern Bengal and parts of Java to the saintliness of individual Muslim devotees who went to live among the infidel, winning them to the faith in the traditional Indian way—by their charisma as holy men.

Christian missionary effort is a specialized, highly organized, and fundamental activity of the Church. It has lapsed when Christianity or a particular Christian church has been on the defensive and thus cut off from missionary opportunities, or when a church has acquired an ethnic or stratal character. These are exceptional circumstances. Christianity has generally seen its frontiers—other than those with Islam—as areas of considerable missionary opportunity and the conversion of populations beyond them as a duty to be carried out by the Church. Christian missionary endeavor is distinctive for its persistence, its centralized organization, and its broad territorial range.

[7] "Let there be no compulsion in religion." (Koran 2:257)

In its early centuries, the Roman Catholic Church performed missionary work directly, putting bishops in charge of converting the northern barbarians while bringing their territories into the hierarchy. This was the nature of the celebrated mission of the Roman bishop, Augustine, sent in the sixth century to convert the pagan Angles and Saxons who had overrun much of previously Christianized Britain. But even then as in later centuries Catholic missionary activity was undertaken by specialized religious orders.

Since the end of the eighteenth century, many Protestant churches have set up mission boards or their equivalent, whose task has been to organize the training and sending of clergymen, both single and married, as preachers of their particular Christian subsystem to some non-Christian population. A distinctive feature of these organizations has been the broad base of financial support they have received from the public in the sending countries.

In the nineteenth century, the expansion of European control over non-European territories, together with developments in transportation, created an unparalleled opportunity for Christian missionary activity. In 1792, the Baptist pastor, William Carey, undertook to appraise the challenge offered to Protestant missionary endeavor by counting the populations adhering to other religions.[8] His estimates, which incorporate some large errors in the data then available, are nevertheless of some interest, and they have been converted in Table 2 to percentages for comparison with current figures.

Table 2. World Population and Religious Affiliation ca. 1790

(in millions)

| | Carey's Estimate ca. 1790 | | |
	Adherents	*Per Cent World Pop.*	*Per Cent 1963 World Pop.* [a]
"Pagans"	420	57.4	47.2
Muslims	130	17.8	14.0
Jews	7	0.9	0.4
Christians	174	23.9	30.0
Catholics	100	13.7	17.7
Eastern Churches	30	4.1	3.6
Protestants	44	6.1	8.7
No religious affiliation, chiefly Christian origin	—	—	8.4
World total	731	100.0	100.0

[a] Total: 3,000.

However, the increase in the number of Christians and of dominantly Christian territories resulting from the missionary effort of the past 150 years is small compared to the growth and expansion of the Christian population of European descent. Missionary efforts had to be directed at individuals on a personal level rather than at large groups as in previous

8 William Carey, *An Inquiry into the Obligations of Christians to Use Means for the Conversion of the Heathens. In Which the Religious State of the Different Nations of the World, the Success of Former Undertakings, and the Practicability of Further Undertakings, are Considered* (Leicester: Ann Ireland, 1792), p. 62. Reprinted by photographic reproduction, London: Baptist Missionary Society, 1934.

centuries. Secularizing trends made Western colonial powers unwilling to assist forcefully in the conversion of subject peoples. Mass conversion of non-European populations, such as had taken place in Spanish America, was a thing of the past.

In fact, of the half million Indians in the United States, "probably less than half that number can be claimed as converts—in any degree—to Christianity," in spite of "prodigious efforts, Protestant and Catholic." [9] Christian Africans comprise approximately half the population in the Eastern Region of Nigeria, an area of great missionary success, but in Ghana and Sierra Leone they comprise only 10 per cent and 3 per cent, respectively. In almost all Asian countries, modern Christian missionary activity has made very modest changes in the religious composition of the population. The greatest changes have occurred in two countries marginal to the area of the Chinese ethnic religion, with their own distinctive ethnic religious mixtures. These are Korea and Vietnam, where Christians comprise 5 per cent and 10 per cent, respectively, of the population.

A significant part of late eighteenth and nineteenth century missionizing in the United States was an internal effort, particularly vigorous because the churches had to gain new members without state support. Sometimes directed indiscriminately at other denominations, it was aimed primarily at those large segments of the population who had lapsed from church-going. The denominations having most success, especially on the frontier, were the Baptists and Methodists, whose ideology and organization in one way or another permitted a religious enthusiasm and improvisation that the Presbyterian and Congregationalist churches did not. Baptists and Methodists also had great success in converting the emancipated Negro population after the Civil War, which represents conversion of a non-European population under very special circumstances.

Geographical Patterns of Interaction Among Religions

The small-scale world map of religions necessarily conceals the occurrence of minority religions as enclaves within larger religious realms and the intermingling of religious communities in transition zones. These patterns, which appear on maps of larger scale, are a product of the processes already described, subject to the different ways religious systems interact with each other.

Interaction among religious systems is of three general types: (1) peaceful coexistence; (2) instability and competition; (3) intolerance and exclusion. In considering these it must be understood that the behavior patterns exhibited are not necessarily a consequence of religious concepts. They may be the product of a long historic experience which lives on in the tradition of the communities involved, even when religious belief and practice are at a low ebb.

PEACEFUL COEXISTENCE. Interaction characterized as "peaceful coexistence" represents an equilibrium, accompanied by mutual feelings of respect, indifference, or antipathy. Simple ethnic religious systems and many elaborate ones, being closely bound to tribe or place, are not con-

[9] Edwin S. Gaustad, *Historical Atlas of Religion in America* (New York: Harper & Row, Publishers, Inc., 1962), p. 144.

cerned with the beliefs and practices of other systems. This is also the pattern of relations among Hindu castes. There is mutual toleration of caste *dharmas,* or moral codes, if only because castes are mutually exclusive communities. A tolerant eclecticism is in turn one of the distinguishing marks of Hinduism's relations with other religious systems. Historical exceptions to this behavior have been largely a reaction to disruption caused by incompatibly exclusive religions.

Broadly speaking, the Oriental religious systems, including the universalizing system, Buddhism, are mutually tolerant. The occasional use of force to repress Buddhism in China, beginning in the ninth century, never resembled the religious persecutions common to Western history.[10] In the Chinese suppression of Mahayana Buddhism, in the harsher repression of Christianity in seventeenth century Japan, and in the expulsion of Jesuit missionaries from China in 1706, the question of the rightness or wrongness of theological beliefs hardly arose. The institutionalized nonproductivity of Buddhist monasteries was considered to be a drain on China's resources and thus a danger to the stability of the state. Similarly, the hardship inflicted on Christianity in later centuries in Japan and China was primarily a response to a supposed challenge to the state.

The mood of religious tolerance which permeates the Oriental world has permitted many people to have a plural religious affiliation. Throughout the Orient, people attend ceremonies at temples of different religious systems. On different occasions during the year, a Chinese might take part in rites performed by Buddhists, Confucianists, Taoists, and ritualists of the folk cults. The ingredients of Oriental religion occur in a fairly uniform blend through the whole cultural territory (Fig. 9A). In Japan, there is no significant regionalization in the distribution of Buddhists and Shintoists such as occurs in the distribution of Protestants in relation to Catholics in Europe, or of Shia Muslims in relation to Sunni Muslims.

Plural religious affiliation was common, too, in the Graeco-Roman world. Christianity's rivals, the popular mystery religions, made no claim to exclusive truth or exclusive fulfillment of an individual's religious needs. The Christian insistence on exclusive truth introduced a new concept into the ideology of universalizing systems, which seems to have provided it with tactical strength.

Another form of coexistence among spatially intermingled religious systems has characterized the Middle East. This is the Ottoman Turkish institution of the *millet.* The term *millet* is the Arabic-Turkish term for "religious community," a legal entity in the Ottoman Empire with virtual autonomy in religious and social matters. Each *millet* had a religious leader who was responsible to the state for the payment of taxes and the observance of public order by the people of his community. In the towns, the *millet* usually occupied a well-defined space often bounded by walls and gates, as was the case in Alexandria, Antioch (Antakya), and Istanbul (Fig. 9B). Jews, Orthodox Greeks, Catholic Armenians, Maronite Christians, and other non-Muslim religious communities had the legal status of *millets.* The non-Sunni Muslim communities were sometimes informally treated in the same way and occupied separate quarters.

[10] C. P. Fitzgerald, *China, a Short Cultural History,* 3rd rev. ed. (New York: Frederick A. Praeger, Inc., 1961), p. 276.

Since these communities were in general fanatically exclusivist in matters of religion, their relatively peaceful coexistence was not accompanied by the religious eclecticism characteristic of the Orient, but it was, despite spatial segregation, marked by political and economic interdependence. Equilibrium among the semiautonomous communities was maintained by the police power of the state, which was Sunni Muslim, the other religious systems being inferior politically. Economically, however, other communities might be far more important than the Sunni. Not uncommonly, individual *millets* would acquire and monopolize different economic specializations, making their regulated coexistence in the towns all the more desirable.

A special two-member case of the *millet* type is the Jewish ghetto in Western Christendom, which had its beginnings at least in the same self-segregating tendency of religious communities that underlies the spatial arrangements of the *millet* system. However, more or less voluntary segregation must be distinguished from the forced confinement to certain districts that characterized ghetto regulation from the sixteenth century to the nineteenth. Moreover, at all times, the Jewish ghetto population in Christendom was subject to far greater insecurity than were the Jewish and Christian *millets* in Muslim lands. In addition to the motive of pollution-avoidance, a certain antipathy among religious communities operates as a powerful self-segregating device. Catholics and Protestants exhibit this tendency in the towns of Northern Ireland, the separation being especially marked in the workingclass districts of Belfast, which tend to be either exclusively Protestant or exclusively Catholic.[11]

The *millet* system increased the internal power of the ecclesiastical organization of each religious community and thus gave them a certain vigor within the rather static framework of the system. In Lebanese and Syrian Christian communities, the bishop is often the arbiter in disputes about marriage, inheritance, and property, and his judgment is rarely challenged by an appeal to the courts. Another legacy of the system is the unusual political power of certain heads of religious organizations, such as Archbishop Makarios of Cyprus.

Another form of tolerant coexistence among religious systems is to be found under the auspices of the secular state, especially where no one church is an established church or predominant in numbers of adherents. The United States represents this condition which has given rise to the denomination. The Protestant denomination is something less than a church in aspiration, for it "assumes only a limited liability for the welfare of its members, leaving great areas of life to society and the state." [12] Moreover, it is one of several religious subsystems each of which has a socially accepted, institutionalized role to play and each of which recognizes the role of others.

So firmly entrenched is this denominational idea in the mind of the American that . . . American Catholics, hardly less than American Protestants or Jews, tend to think of their church as a denomination existing side by side

[11] M. W. Heslinga, *The Irish Border as a Cultural Divide* (Assen: van Gorcum, 1962), p. 66.
[12] Gaustad, *Historical Atlas*, p. 113, citing Sidney E. Mead, "Denominationalism: the Shape of Protestantism in America," *Church History*, XXIII (1954).

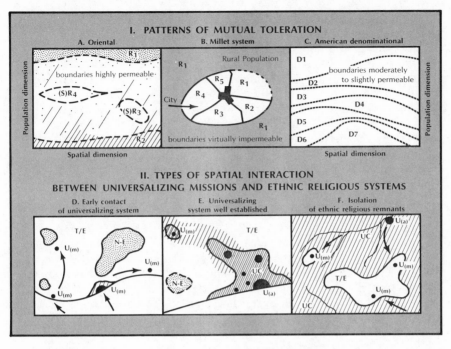

I. PATTERNS OF MUTUAL TOLERATION

A. Oriental B. Millet system C. American denominational

II. TYPES OF SPATIAL INTERACTION
BETWEEN UNIVERSALIZING MISSIONS AND ETHNIC RELIGIOUS SYSTEMS

D. Early contact of universalizing system E. Universalizing system well established F. Isolation of ethnic religious remnants

D Denomination	tribal) religion
N-E Neo-ethnic, messianic religion or religious movement	**U** Universalizing religion
R Religious system	**U(a)** Administrative center of universalizing system
(S)R Syncretistic "new" religion or sect	**UC** Converts to universalizing religion
T/E Weakly organized ethnic (including	**U(m)** Missionary establishment

FIG. 9. *Patterns of interaction among religions.*

with other denominations in a pluralistic harmony that is felt to be somehow of the texture of American life.[13]

The American circumstances that gave rise to this complex of denominational subsystems include such elements as regional diversity in church affiliation in the colonial period, the absence of an established church at the time of the country's founding, the mobile nature of the population, both spatially and socially, and the diversity of churches represented in the waves of nineteenth century immigrants from Europe. The institutionalizing of the denomination has involved a lessening, if not a complete cessation, of intergroup proselytizing, in contrast to the dynamically unstable situation in the first eighty years or so of the country's existence; it is now only the newer sects (Mormonism, Jehovah's Witnesses, etc.) which proselytize among other Christian communities.

Distinctive spatial relationships arise in the American situation, and the regional predominance of one religious community is the exception. It is, in fact, only found in the Mormon country and in certain old Catholic areas such as French Louisiana and the Rio Grande Valley. Elsewhere there is spatial coexistence of two or more numerically substantial

[13] Will Herberg, *Protestant-Catholic-Jew* (New York: Doubleday & Company, Inc., 1955), p. 86.

denominations and usually many minor ones, which tend to be associated in a social stratification (Fig. 9C). Thus in approximately one-half of the counties in the country, no single religious body accounts for more than 50 per cent of all the membership in the county.[14]

The evolution of denominationalism in the late eighteenth and nineteenth centuries was marked by a phase of active fission. The reaction to this has been the regrouping of religious bodies into larger systems, an aspect of the process termed ecumenism. As yet, there has been only a consolidation of certain denominations and the creation of a mood of collaboration among religious organizations, rather than a major restructuring of any of the larger Christian subsystems. Some of this consolidation has evidently had quite practical motives: to effect economies of scale, to achieve what can be best described as greater class solidarity, and, in some cases, to renounce finally the ethnicity which had kept a religious body separate.

On a broader scale, ecumenism refers to a movement toward greater collaboration among Christian religious systems that received its impetus from the need to cooperate in missionary work. From it has come the World Council of Churches, an association of many Protestant bodies together with a number of Eastern Orthodox churches. This association does not involve its members in a merger or union as religious bodies. Ecumenical associations of this type also link the national branches of Protestant denominations such as the Presbyterians. The ecumenism of these movements has not so far shown signs of successfully developing an effective supranational outlook or extending deep roots into the masses of the congregations represented.

While the Roman Catholic Church has recently evinced an interest in ecumenism, its program is carried out on its own terms. Its Ecumenical Council (Vatican II) was primarily concerned with airing matters of internal concern to the Church. There was also debate on the relations of the Church with other religious systems, discussing, for example, the possibility of common worship with Protestants under special circumstances.

COMPETITION AND INSTABILITY. A different kind of interaction among religious systems is a competitive one, in which one of the systems is characterized by instability. A high incidence of contact conversion and missionary activity is associated with this condition. The expansion of Europeans, from the fifteenth century on, brought Christianity into close contact with many other religious systems. In the contact with Christianity, the simple ethnic religions have exhibited the greatest instability. This effect decreases progressively in the Christian contact with the Indian ethnic system, the East Asian ethnic systems, and Buddhism, and virtually disappears in the contact with Islam.

Outside the ancient zone of conflict between Islam and Christianity (Fig. 5), there has never been much conversion of Muslims to Chris-

[14] Gaustad, *op. cit.*, p. 159. Gaustad gives the statement a different emphasis to show the departure from the American standard of well-intermingled denominations. At the local level of township and village in parts of the Midwest, individual denominations often attain a high degree of dominance.

tianity or vice versa. However, these two systems have been in active competition as a result of their common contacts with other religions, chiefly simple tribal religions in the Indonesian, Indian, and African areas. In Africa, the Islamic and Christian absorption of simple tribal religions is bringing the two universalizing systems into closer contact along a front coinciding with the savanna/forest boundary south of the Sahara. This confrontation is already contributing, as it formerly did in the Malayan realm, to political tension.

Christianity has had to adapt to varying political and economic relationships between East and West in its competition with the Oriental religions, as is shown by the use of several different missionary strategies vis-à-vis those religions. Preceding the industrial development of Europe, a tentative Christian strategy was to preach to the elites of the high civilizations of the Orient in terms of their own traditions and practices. This approach was frustrated by the reluctance of church authorities to approve an "Asianizing" of what were often merely European cultural accretions on the body of Christianity. However, Catholic missions have usually been more flexible in accepting cultural modifications of European Christian practice as a missionary strategy than have the less catholic propagandists of Protestant denominations.

A different strategy used by Christian missionaries has been to concentrate effort at the more unstable lower social and economic levels. The technique has certain disadvantages. In India, for instance, the segmented nature of society permitted Christian missionaries to make sweeping conversions among discrete segments of the economically and socially depressed classes. Because Indian society is rigidly stratified, missionary success at the lower social levels tended to retard the upward spread of Christianity. As a religion associated with the lowest castes, it might be denigrated by the upper, who would consider it inappropriate for them.

In China, the association of Christianity with the people of the West generally inhibited the Christian effort. Exceptions to the xenophobic resistance to Christianity occurred among the class of "new men" who had more to gain from business and political dealings with the West than from the preservation of the old order. Religious instability has been greater among Chinese and Japanese exposed to Christianity outside their Far Eastern homelands. In the United States, about one-fifth of first generation Japanese and slightly over a half of the second generation were Christians in 1931, although even in the 1950's only 7 to 8 per cent of the American population of Chinese descent had been converted.

Economic imbalance as reflected in the difference between the living standards of the Brazilian masses and of rich Brazilians and North Americans in general has been successfully exploited in recent decades by American Protestant missionary organizations. There are now around four million Protestants in dominantly Catholic Brazil, mostly "from the lower classes," with a few middle-class converts in the cities.[15] One consequence of conversion to Protestantism, however, is a change in world view as well as certain material changes, such as an increase in literacy; lower-

[15] Kenneth S. Latourette, *History of Expansion of Christianity*, Vol. 7 (New York: Harper & Row, Publishers, Inc., 1945), p. 182.

class converts have shown a tendency to gravitate upward into the middle class.[16]

Political dissension, especially in an area dominated by an ethnic religious system, may promote religious instability. The temporary successes of Christianity in sixteenth century Japan are in part attributed to the tension beween the center and the southern provinces, where Christianity made most of its advance. However, the central regime was able to stifle the southern discontent and then attempted to eradicate Christianity on the grounds that it had contributed to the dissension.

Interaction causing instability in a religious system may result not in an overt transfer of adherence, but in such a large transfer of religious culture as to constitute a disguised conversion. Many elements of an alien religious system may be adopted, but not the alien identity. Resistance to a change in identity is usually associated with an ethnic or quasiethnic ideal and antipathy toward the other system because of historical experiences. The American Indians choosing Peyotism rather than Christianity because of the association of Christianity with the Whites is a case in point. The resistance of Judaism to Christianity in modern times has an analogous character, although American Judaism has been significantly affected in its organization by its contact with Protestantism. Reform Judaism, which has eliminated much ritual and the liturgical use of Hebrew, is a product of this interaction.

The reverse behavior appears when rapid, if nominal, conversion to a universalizing system takes place, perhaps under the momentary threat of force: a new religious identity is accepted but this conceals the retention of much of the old religion. The equilibrium is in fact not disturbed enough to allow a deep transformation of religious ideas and values. In Java, elements of the folk religion were given an Islamic veneer; in India, a fundamental Christian and Islamic social ethic has been altered by the persistence of caste in Christian and Muslim Indian society; and in Latin America, the Catholic compromise with some form of aboriginal practice was openly conceded when, after a few disastrous attempts, the scrutiny of the Inquisition was not applied to the Indians, who were nominally Christians.

One consequence of interaction along a front marked by moderate instability is the generation of new syncretic religions. Sikhism, for example, is a crystallization of one of several syncretisms arising from the interaction of Islam and Hinduism. Other syncretic forms have arisen along the front of interaction between Christianity, or a Christianizing Western civilization, and the religious systems of the Orient. Among these are the messianic religion preached by the Taiping rebels in the midnineteenth century; Caodaism in South Vietnam; Chondo-kyo, a Korean religion started in 1859 by an apostate from Catholicism.

In the encounter between Christianity and simple ethnic systems, one reaction on the part of the latter is an intensification of conservatism, which may succeed in preserving stability for a while, as it appears to have done among the Hopi. Another is the generation of prophetic salvation movements. The same cultural loss and sense of inadequate identity

[16] Emilio Willems, "Protestantism as a Factor in Culture Change in Brazil," *Economic Development and Culture Change*, III (1954-55), 321-33.

which may precede conversion to the universalizing system are felt, but conversion to Christianity is not attractive because it seems difficult and perhaps impossible to achieve economic and social identity with the representatives of Christendom.

While messianic and prophet-salvation cults are a local reaction to stress from the impact of western Christian civilization on simple religions, some elements of these cults have a wide distribution. Certain traits occur within a broad culture region—western United States, West Africa, South Africa, Melanesia. Each of these is a diffusion field in which certain distinctive elements, like the "ghost dance" of the North American Indians and the "cargo" of good things awaited by the Melanesians, appear frequently in the ideology and myth of the region's cults. The essential cargo myth has appeared in many different places along hundreds of miles of sparsely populated Melanesian coasts and island chains.

The distribution of prophet-salvation movements, breaking out sporadically among certain segments of a much disturbed simple society under colonial rule, expresses the geographic pattern associated with the front of interaction among religious systems (Fig. 9D). Missionary organization and drive then tend to create a pattern of nuclear cells having finger-like extensions, with a penumbra of scantier adherence around the core concentrations (Fig. 9E). The map of Christianity in southern Asia, particularly if differentiated by social level, would disclose this pattern. In an advanced stage of interaction, the earlier cores will have coalesced, and the front is expressed by the shredded pattern of the religion in retreat, with here and there a compact island of resistance (Fig. 9F). Such a pattern would be seen on a large-scale map of Middle and South America which showed the position of the Catholic advance against the simple religions of the Indian population.

INTOLERANCE. The practice of an exclusivist religious intolerance comprises the third general type of interaction among religious systems. While Oriental religious systems are pervaded by attitudes of permissiveness or indifference to other religions, each of the religions of the western Old World—Judaism, Christianity, and Islam—has historically exhibited hostility toward all other religions. This attitude, creating communities of believers making claims to the exclusive possession of religious truth and, derivatively, of social truth, has at times provoked a hostile reaction among adherents of Oriental religious systems. The militancy of Sikhs and Hindus in the Punjab was in large part a reaction to the militancy of Islam there, just as the recent political aggressiveness of Buddhists in South Vietnam has been the counterpart of vigorous political self-expression by Christian communities. Altogether, the record of religious intolerance in many lands has been a long, dreary, and often horrible one: "tantum religio potuit suadere malorum." [17]

Where religious orthodoxy prevails by force, the map of religions shows a pattern of homogeneous blocks with sharp boundaries marking the limits of a religious authority. Even long after the intolerance of an earlier age has subsided, the abrupt geographical transition from the pre-

[17] "So many evils has religion provoked." Lucretius, De rerum natura (On the Nature of Things).

dominance of one religious system to another most often records some earlier intransigence (Fig. 10).

The nature of simple ethnic religious systems is such that mutual tolerance is hardly in question. A form of intolerance appeared in the relations between ancient state religious systems, whose fate often followed the fortunes of war. In the ancient Middle East, ethnic gods would be struck down as a result of conquest by foreign armies. They might then be abandoned by their followers, the sway of new ethnic gods being extended over the conquered territories. However, the marked abhorrence of bloodshed in northern India, where Buddhism originated, ruled out the use of conquest and violence as means of propagating that religion, and this idea in turn permeated much of southern and eastern Asia.

Very little of this Oriental attitude appears even in the ideology of the Western universalizing religions. The idea of a violent external struggle between opposing forces (Good and Evil) has Babylonian roots, becoming more specific in Zoroastrianism, which in turn influenced post-exilic Judaism. Toynbee is inclined to derive the peculiarly intolerant elements in operative Christianity, which occur to a lesser extent in Islam, from features present in Judaism of the pre-Christian period.[18] Whether or not Judaism was influenced in this respect by the Persian world-view, its exclusivist features seem to be largely an extension of a different idea. This is the idea that the sacred and the polluted must be kept apart, particularly in their spatial expression.

The spatial relationships resulting from the insistence on this separation are to be seen on a small scale in Hindu caste society. The orthodox Brahman seeks to exclude pollution-bearing lower castes from his home and from his quarter in the village. At one time in South India, menials of the lowest social strata had not only to reside some distance from the village occupied by the high castes and to take water from a separate well, but also to keep out of their way, and in extreme cases out of their sight. In Israel of the Old Testament period, the religious practices of other ethnic groups were seen as conveying the same kind of defilement. They were therefore to be eradicated from the territory considered sacred. Failing this, they were to be avoided and anathematized. Such a relationship with other religious communities would be uncomfortable enough; embodied in the ideology of universalizing Christianity, it had disastrous consequences, and for none more so than the Jews.

The Zoroastrian rulers of Persia used political power to impose their religious system on their subjects and succeeded in assuring its dominance within the confines of their state. The same kind of success followed the forceful imposition of Christianity, then a minority religion, on the people of the Roman Empire at the end of the fourth century. The earlier coexistence of competing systems of belief and worship came to an end with the evolution of a cosmopolitan religious society whose members not only saw its message as applicable to all mankind, but in addition saw themselves as a "distinct people . . . hostile to other religions; they declared that they had final truth and would eliminate rival faiths." [19]

The use of political pressure to destroy rival faiths was supplemented

[18] *Study of History,* Vol. 6, pp. 38-49; Vol. 7, p. 438.
[19] Latourette, *op. cit.,* Vol. 1, p. 128.

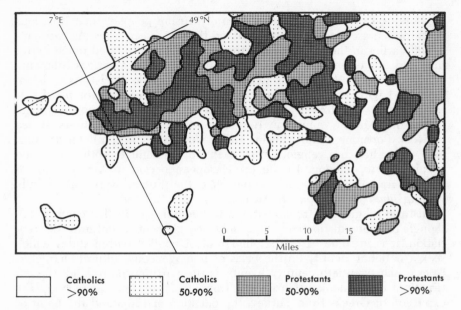

FIG. 10. *Distribution of Catholics and Protestants in central Europe: an example from Alsace-Lorraine, ca. 1910. (Adapted from Georg Wolfram and Werner Gley,* Elsass-Lothringischer Atlas. *Frankfurt-am-Main: Elsass-Lothringischer Institut, 1931.)*

by the destruction of other religious systems through conquest and the extension of political controls inducing conversion through a variety of pressures. To this end, Christian religious systems have conducted numerous campaigns of violence against other religions and against heretical doctrines that have arisen internally. Even the coexistence of denominations that is now so characteristically American was not present in the beginning. Puritan New England zealously practised exclusivism and intolerance, employing the full police power of the state to attack religious deviation. The principle of individual religious freedom was only established in 1663 in the northern colonies, when Roger Williams founded the Providence Plantation in what is now Rhode Island.

Islam's extension of its domain by war on nonbelievers follows the policy enunciated in the Islamic tradition. There is *dār al-Islām,* the Islamic realm, and *dār al-ḥarb,* "the land of warfare," that is, the field in which Islam has to contest with other religions for dominance. To wage war of this kind has been a sacred obligation. Wars arising from political and economic conflict between Muslim nations and Christian or Hindu powers have been declared *jihād,* or "holy war." The rapid expansion of Muslim power in the seventh century was an expression of this policy. Christian and Zoroastrian lands in the Middle East were overrun by the armies of Islam, but the conquered populations were with few exceptions allowed to continue in their own religion as politically subordinate communities. In fact, there was little fanaticism toward the non-Muslim "people of the book," and Christians occupied high office. In time, however, the deference paid to Christianity began to wear thin.

A second phase of military expansion having permanent results was the conquest of India by a succession of Muslim peoples, their invasions reaching a crescendo in the twelfth and thirteenth centuries. As had happened earlier in the Middle East, the pre-Muslim elite fared much better than did, for example, the pre-Christian elite in the Americas following Christian conquest in the sixteenth century. In Southeast Asia, Islam took hold without military campaigns. There the concept of *jihād* was revived in a desultory way when the Western Christian powers penetrated this Muslim sphere in the sixteenth century. Encounters at sea between Portuguese and Muslim Malay ships had the character of guerrilla skirmishes in a religious war; each side thought the other accursed because of its religion. In the pre-European period in Africa south of the Sahara, Muslim Negro peoples like the Fulani were successfully waging *jihād* against pagan Africans.

Historic religious hatreds continue to bedevil man in this century. Although religious distinctiveness is only one element of cultural differentiation, it is in some cases the chief root of conflict within states which seek a national identity on the basis of homogeneous cultural characteristics. Such twentieth century events as the partition of Ireland, the extirpation of Armenian Christians from their ancient homeland, the expulsion of Greeks from Turkey, the partition of India and the flight of millions of people as a result, the continuing crises involving Cyprus, Israel, Kashmir, Ceylon, and South Vietnam, all show how nationalist ideologies have not been able to tolerate religious diversity. Nationalism itself, having arisen in the West, seems to have inherited in full measure the legacy of Western religious intolerance.

Dynamism of Universalizing Religious Systems

A comparison of the growth of the three major universalizing systems suggests certain conclusions about the relative dynamism associated with different techniques of expansion and modes of interaction with other systems. The first to achieve permanence as the prevailing system of a religious realm was Theravada Buddhism. This gave rise, probably in northwestern India, to the Mahayana system, which moved into most of eastern Asia, but could not penetrate the barrier of Zoroastrianism to the west.

Buddhist expansion from 300 B.C. to A.D. 700 was uneven. The system achieved acceptance for the most part only in certain influential strata of society and while advancing on the periphery, failed to maintain itself in its hearth area. The realm that survives (see Fig. 6) occupies only a fraction of Buddhism's former sphere of influence, and has been relatively static for the past millennium. Mahayana Buddhism had for long a large following and great influence, but it has been displaced by or absorbed into the ethnic religious systems of East Asia. It has also become the quasi-ethnic system of Tibetan Lamaism, contributing a late flicker of competitive dynamism in Buddhism's history by reaching out to convert the pagan nomadic peoples to the north.

Buddhism's development of the monastic community as the circulatory medium of a universalizing religious system was a unique advance in systems of religious organization, and its separation of religious and mundane society permitted it to be dynamic and, to a certain extent, popular. But this separation meant that it was weakly based. Other systems which have depended primarily on monastic institutions, such as Manichaeism and, less so, the Eastern Orthodox Church, have proved vulnerable to displacement under moderate social or economic stress. On the whole, Buddhism has evidently been less dynamic and less resistant to pressure than the other major universalizing systems because of its renunciation of force as a political instrument.

In tracing the growth of Christianity, one is in fact dealing with the evolution of several systems, among which radical organizational differences have arisen in time. Christianity's initial period of expansion in four main institutional branches between the second and sixth centuries was followed by a severe setback—the loss in the seventh century of most of the Southwest Asian and North African provinces of Christendom to the dominion of a suddenly emergent Islam. From the ninth century to the fourteenth, Christianity advanced northward and eastward in the European lands outside the former territory of the Roman Empire, but simultaneously toward the latter part of that period, Christian populations in Asia Minor and southeastern Europe were coming under Muslim rule, and more losses of Christian communities by conversion to Islam took place, chiefly in Asia Minor.

The expansion of European influence far beyond its boundaries enabled the Christian realm to grow to primacy in both area and population by the end of the nineteenth century. Since then, apart from the rise of secularism and quasi-religious systems such as Communism, political changes have put a brake on Christian missionary activity in many areas. It is estimated that continuation of present rates of population change alone will have reduced the proportion of Christians, including the most nominal, to about one-fifth of the world population by the year 2000.

The traditional church that has remained dynamic through many centuries of vicissitudes is the Roman Catholic Church. At times its organizational framework has tended to become ossified and cumbersome, but the specialized religious orders have repeatedly restored vitality by stimulating technological innovation, by advancing pioneer settlement, and by propagating the system among non-Christian peoples. Its militant exclusiveness and its use of force to establish the religion and maintain conformity at certain periods seem to have been tactical advantages. Its increasing emphasis on catholicity suggests that its primacy among Christian subsystems will increase, despite such inroads as those recently made by Protestantism in Latin America.

Protestantism has sought to broaden the base of religious participation by the community at large, so that ideally the whole society is enrolled in the religious life. An element in this program is the cultivation of literacy, which in turn has been an essential ingredient of a vigorously growing society. Innovativeness in forms of organization has become characteristic, and while this has helped to involve a larger fraction of society, it has created many virtually independent subsystems. Taken as a whole, the Protestant set of subsystems has a narrower ethnic base than the Catholic Church, quite apart from the ethnicity manifested by national organisms like the Church of England. Preponderantly, the Protestant community is of northern European stock, the major exceptions being the formerly "client" Negro populations in North America and South Africa. The growth and prosperity of the Protestant realm, the result of complex economic processes, have contributed to its missionary appeal.

Islam also assigns the full responsibility for a religious life to the individual. Despite the absence of a church and formal missionary institutions, it has the advantage of seeing itself as a single community. This fellowship seems to have been a powerful cement. It has served to consolidate the gains achieved by a policy of conquest and relative tolerance combined with the kind of material prosperity and prestige that have helped Protestantism to grow. In its direct confrontation with Christianity, it has had on balance by far the greater success (Fig. 5).

In the fifteenth century, Islam was the most widely distributed religious system in the world. It bestrode the land mass of the Old World, controlling the major routes of east-west movement and mediating the flow of culture along them. After the European powers challenged its control of those routes, its fortunes changed. Yet while the economic and political decline within the Arab hearth continued, Muslim states in Persia, India, and Turkey achieved new vigor. On the periphery, in Central Asia, Indonesia, and West Africa, many new converts were gained. Since then Islam has lost much ground politically and with it the means of attracting outsiders in large numbers. Its experience in the last two centuries has been the reverse of Protestantism's: the relative economic and technological decline of much of the Muslim world has deprived Islam of one of its former attractions. Its tenacity in this period of political and economic eclipse has been all the more striking: in the past three centuries the number of Muslim converts to Christianity has remained minuscule.

Toward the end of the eighteenth century, a Congregational divine observed in connection with the contemporary increase in Baptist membership: if numbers were taken as proof of religious truth, think what this would declare about "the Papists," to say nothing of "the peculiar sentiments of Mahomet." [20] This plaintive deprecation of numbers makes a valid point: numbers of adherents alone cannot suggest the historical significance of a religious system or the meaning it can have in the lives of individuals. Christianity and Islam have together so dominated the religious historical traditions of Western civilization that we may need to be reminded that just under half of the people now living in the world have no tradition of affiliation with either of these systems. The conquests and conversions of many centuries still allow us to discern beneath the gross distribution pattern of religions in the Old World the ghostly pattern of the world as it was 2,500 to 3,000 years ago. The Aegean-Mediterranean hearth of Europa, the riverine cores of Dry World civilization, the Middle Ganges center of Indic civilization, and the Chinese hearth are still visible, each the focal area of a contemporary religious realm.

[20] Cited in Gaustad, *Historical Atlas*, p. 12.

contemporary religion— geographic considerations

So far, the question of fidelity of belief and practice among those who "have a religion" has been circumvented. The behavior of each religious community has been considered without regard to the convictions of all those brought up in the shared tradition of a particular religion. However, fidelity is critical for the vitality of religious systems. Too, the role of contemporary quasi-religious systems of political faith should be considered. These can displace traditional religions as a social guiding force, although they do not always do so overtly.

Patterns of Adherence

Data about religious fidelity are mostly qualitative and impressionistic, often providing only superficial indices such as the degree of observance of food taboos. For western, particularly Protestant, countries, various indications available for the past two centuries have been used to estimate the patterns of religious adherence. Hume's midnineteenth century "Religious Map of England," adapted as Figure 11, p. 109, is an early example of a map showing patterns of adherence as well as of confession.[1]

In the eighteenth century, a spirit of rationalism, involving a questioning of traditional religious beliefs, had spread in western Europe both as the aftermath of the religious wars of the previous century and as the consequence of a rapid expansion of knowledge about man and his world. Of the general population in that age, many felt a fatigued indifference to traditional religion. Thus it was not simply freedom of reli-

[1] A. Hume, *Remarks on the Census of Religious Worship for England and Wales, with Suggestions for an Improved Census in 1861, and a Map, Illustrating the Religious Condition of the Country* (London: Longmans, Green, Longmans & Roberts, 1860).

gion that was sought in eighteenth century North America. Many wanted a freedom from religion in the sense of a formally organized system of religious beliefs and practices. Whatever their private beliefs, most Americans went without membership in a church. In 1800, it is estimated, church membership did not embrace more than one-sixth of the population.[2] Soon after, Protestant denominations began to recruit members actively, while immigration from Europe brought many who maintained their church affiliation. By 1900, about a third of the population were members of a church, and the proportion is now nearly two-thirds.

Religious involvement by denomination varies greatly, according to current estimates based mostly on church membership and attendance. Catholicism commands an especially high level of participation in the life of the Church, approximately 70 per cent of American Catholics attending regularly. Since most of them live in cities and industrial towns, their observance contrasts remarkably with the slight participation of the urban-industrial populace in European Catholic countries. Data for other American communities suggest that the proportion of regular participants is 45 per cent among Negroes, 35 per cent among White Protestants, and 17 per cent among Jews. For the Jews, other criteria show even lower levels of traditional religious observance.[3] Among major Protestant denominations, Episcopalians have the lowest attendance record, Baptists the highest.

Although the current church "boom" is in part socially motivated, there is at the same time much thinking and experimenting with new religious forms in western Christianity. Catholic worker-priest missions, Protestant ventures into monastic life, attempts to return to primitive Christian communal worship in city apartment buildings, the groping toward ecumenism, and the movement of *aggiornamento* ("updating") in the Catholic Church are all part of a search for contemporary meaning in traditional religion.

In America, social identification with some religious system is more prevalent than the estimates of religious fidelity suggest. About 97 per cent of the population in the United States belong to some formal religious system. The identification tends to be stable and is often a precise indicator of cultural and social origins.[4]

In most of the other technologically advanced countries, the massive displacements of population associated with industrialization and the conditions of urban life have reinforced popular disenchantment with the established religions. Both Protestants and Catholics in western Europe, especially in the industrial regions, have low levels of adherence.

[2] Kenneth S. Latourette, *History of the Expansion of Christianity*, Vol. 4 (New York: Harper & Row, Publishers, Inc., 1941), p. 177; Will Herberg, *Protestant-Catholic-Jew* (New York: Doubleday & Company, Inc., 1955), pp. 48, 66n. W. Zelinsky, "An Approach to the Religious Geography of the United States," *Annals*, Association of American Geographers, LI (1961), 148n., contends that church membership in 1775-76 could have been as high as 48 per cent of the total population, but Gaustad's data on the average size of various congregations at that period show this to have been unlikely. See Edwin S. Gaustad, *Historical Atlas of Religion in America* (New York: Harper & Row, Publishers, Inc., 1962), pp. 11, 12, 16, 162.

[3] Marshall Sklare, *The Jews: Social Patterns of an American Group* (New York: Free Press of Glencoe, Inc., 1958); C. B. Sherman, *The Jew Within American Society* (Detroit: Wayne State University Press, 1961).

[4] Cf. Andrew H. Clark, "Old World Origins and Religious Adherence in Nova Scotia," *Geographical Review*, L (1960), 317-44.

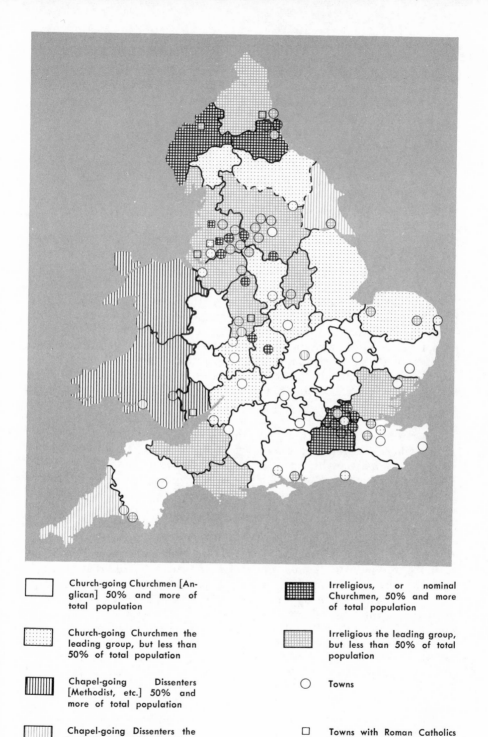

FIG. 11. *Religious adherence in England and Wales,* ca. 1850. *(Based on Dr. Hume's "Religious Map of England," 1860.)*

Proportionally, many more Europeans than Americans disavow affiliation with religious systems. In 1950, 17 per cent of the Dutch population did so.[5] In Scandinavia, the Lutheran churches do enroll almost everyone, but participation and interest in religion are much lower than among American Protestants.[6] About 35 per cent of the population of Japan admits to "believing in" any one of the traditional religions, whereas in the United States, 80 to 95 per cent of the population, depending on the criteria used, do so.

In the Soviet Union and most Communist countries, the majority of the population would seem to have no belief in any of the traditional religions, partly because the Communist establishment tries to discredit them and restricts their operations. This need not mean that people there subscribe to the quasi religion of the Marxist-Leninist state with any more conviction than that shown by western Europeans with respect to Christianity.

In France, church-supported social geographic studies, under the name of "religious sociology," have had the aim of measuring, mapping, and interpreting the regional variations in Catholic adherence and observance.[7] While less than 5 per cent of people of Catholic descent openly disavow the Church to the extent of refusing such rites as baptism and burial, 60 per cent rarely have contact with it; the remaining 35 per cent practice with some regularity. Boulard's study differentiates between the participation of adults and minors, and establishes criteria for three categories of popular commitment to the Church (Fig. 12). These may be summarized as "actively participating," "passive," and "defecting." In the latter category, 20 per cent or more of the Catholic population by origin deliberately remain outside the Church.

The Church considers areas of defection to be "mission areas," which must be approached by agencies and techniques outside the means of the ordinary territorial hierarchy. Boulard does not discuss the level of "service" provided by the territorial hierarchy, but it is obviously related to the level of participation (see Fig. 4). A falling away from the Church reduces the local resources of money and manpower, and this, in turn, weakens the ability of the Church to hold people's allegiance. Conservatively rural areas, like Brittany, Gascony, and the Cevennes, are staunchly Catholic; the industrial zones and major conurbations are areas of defection. The precise relationships are more complex, and trends going back as far as pre-Revolution days may affect adherence. Rationalist influences emanating from Paris seem already to have been sapping the vigor of the Church in rural areas of the Paris Basin in the eighteenth century. With the individualization and commercialization of farming there, indifference to the Church showed a marked increase, so that even the environs of Chartres and its splendid cathedral have had to be designated a mission area. A study of attendance at mass shows different levels of

[5] Imbrighi, *Lineamenti di geografia religiosa* (Rome: Editrice Studium, 1961), p. 79.
[6] Eric Fisher, "Religions: Their Distribution and Role in Political Geography," in *Principles of Political Geography,* ed. Hans W. Weigert *et al.* (New York: Appleton-Century-Crofts, 1957), p. 407.
[7] Fernand Boulard, *An Introduction to Religious Sociology: Pioneer Work in France,* trans. M. J. Jackson (London: Darton, Longman & Todd, Ltd., 1960). Studies in social microgeography have also been done at the parish and diocese levels.

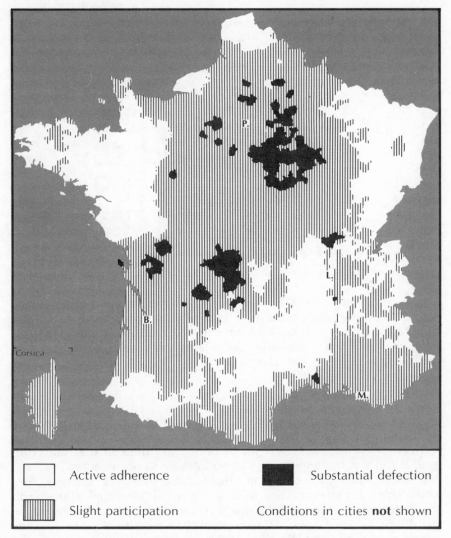

Active adherence   Substantial defection

Slight participation   Conditions in cities **not** shown

FIG. 12. *Catholic adherence in rural France*, ca. 1950. *(Figures 12 and 13 adapted from Boulard,* An Introduction to Religious Sociology.)

participation on either side of the Franco-Belgian border, with attendance consistently higher on the Belgian side (Fig. 13). The contrast is less marked just inland from the coast where there is an unusually high level of attendance in the Flemish-speaking area of northwestern France.[8] These French studies show how the paths of circulation of ideas, the existence of culture areas as distinct fields of communication, and regional differences in the spatial organization of religious systems can affect the vitality of a religion.

Herberg suggests that current religious activity in the United States

---

[8] Boulard, *op. cit.*, pp. 66-70.

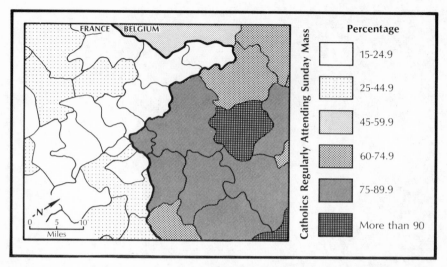

FIG. 13. *Attendance at mass on the Franco-Belgian border. Data by parishes.*

surpasses that of western Europe, where indifference to formal religion is more widespread, because it is part of the contemporary American popular faith that religion—any institutional religion—is a good thing.[9] A tolerant coexistence pervades the relationships among even the most firmly ethnic religions and churches.

Quasi-religious Systems

The unifying American faith is a faith in the American Way of Life and is built on the idealized concept of the new order of things that was and is to obtain in the New World.[10] Americans think of it as universalizing because it has appeared to be so in the American context, successfully subordinating the claims of ethnic and credal particularisms. In a world context, however, it is seen to be a culture-bound ethnic faith which cannot be acquired by simple verbal acceptance. For example, one distinguishing mark of ethnic systems, the sanctity of place, is made manifest in the extraordinarily elaborate efforts often devoted to the return of American dead to the national soil.

The faith in the American Way of Life is only a special case of various nationalisms that have taken on the character of ethnic systems of faith. "There is in nationalism a religious element or, better, nationalism is in a sense a religion in itself." [11] The view that some integrating social systems, such as nationalism and Communism, are in fact religions is becoming increasingly common, since they seem to conform to most comprehensive definitions of a religion, including the requirement of a faith in ideas that are beyond empirical demonstration.[12] For some, it

---

[9] Herberg, *Protestant-Catholic-Jew*. This is a major theme of the book.
[10] *Ibid.*, p. 80.
[11] Jan Romein, *The Asian Century: a History of Modern Nationalism in Asia* (London: George Allen & Unwin, Ltd., 1962), p. 30.
[12] See, e.g., J. Paul Williams, "The Nature of Religion," *Journal for the Scientific Study of Religion,* II (1962), 3-14.

must be pointed out, what disqualifies them as religions is the absence of worship. But whether or not these modern systems of belief are called religions, as they are by many, for geographical purposes they can be treated exactly as if they are religious systems and can be analyzed in the same way as traditional ones. For convenience, we may refer to them as quasi religions.

Nationalist faith involves a belief in the supreme importance of the nation. Some communities may already have a traditional ethnic religious system, and when nationalism flourishes with attainment of the appropriate economic and educational levels, the traditional ethnic religion can become an important ingredient in the new nationalism. Shinto transformed into the Japanese nationalist religion in the nineteenth century is the classic example. A formal nationalist quasi religion can be invented, as happened in Nazi Germany.

Nationalist quasi religions assign a transcending importance, approaching sanctity, to certain elements in the material world. The use by nationalist quasi religions of the term "sacred," as in Italian exaltation of *sacro egoismo*, or as in that cliché of nationalist iconography, the "sacred soil of the fatherland," is by no means simply metaphorical.

Competing with such ethnically oriented quasi religions as the faith in the American Way of Life is a truly universalizing quasi religion, Communism. This system has grown and spread by the same processes as the traditional religious systems. It has had specific effects on the land, it is territorially organized, and it interacts with other quasi religions and with the traditional religions as well. There are, in particular, a number of parallels between Christianity and Communism as two vehicles of universalizing religious-philosophical ideas, however different the two sets of ideas may be.

Since Communism arose in a society impregnated with the Christian tradition, it has certain religious features derived from that tradition. The myth of the redeeming role of the proletariat, ushering in the Golden Age, is one which "takes over and continues one of the great eschatological myths of the Asiatico-Mediterranean world." [13] In its ethos of work and sacrifice, there is an element of Protestant asceticism. It has the militantly exclusivist attitudes of the Western universalizing religions and the same concept of a dualistic struggle between Good and Evil from which, in part, this exclusivism is ultimately derived.

In Communism, because it is a quasi-religious system of a materialist kind, worship is absent, although there are rites such as the annual May Day celebration. It has its revered teachers and scriptures, sacrosanct in that they may not be confuted but can be circumvented by skillful casuistry. For a universalizing system, the absence of a sacred focus and a sacred language can be an asset, provided an adequate communications network exists. Because of the European milieu of early Marxism, however, an unsubordinated ethnic differentiation is present internally and may lead to a schism between dominantly European and dominantly

---

[13] Mircea Eliade, *The Sacred and the Profane* (New York: Harper & Row, Publishers, Inc., 1961), p. 206. Erich Isaac, "Religion, Landscape, and Space," *Landscape*, IX (Winter 1960), 18, points out that a contemporary study of the *religious* motive at work in transforming the land may be appropriately directed to the cultural landscape of the present day as it is related to the ideology of the prevailing materialist quasi religions.

non-European factions, comparable to the regional schisms that occurred within Christianity.

The ecological circumstance which enabled Communism to spread was the existence of a worldwide communication and transportation network and a Europe-dominated imperium, with the industrialized (capitalist) West at its core. Communism did not confine its original message to a particular ethnic group but appeared from the beginning as a universalizing system; "Workers of the world, unite!" Adherents of Communism organized cells of belief and proselytization in urban industrial centers. Members were drawn from socially and economically depressed classes, foreign ethnic groups, and a sprinkling of dissident philosophers. Subject to repression, its followers have "gone underground," a phrase recalling the catacombs of Rome. Invested with political power in a large empire, Communism used force in an attempt to root out heretical belief and practice, although at times compromising with custom, particularly among the peasantry.

Communism has expanded and defended its domain through warfare, victory being followed by the application of pressure to induce conversion. By various means Communism has made substantial inroads into a number of the great religious realms, supplanting Christian churches over wide areas and absorbing, or profoundly transforming, the ethnic religious system of the Chinese, as none of the universalizing religions, including Buddhism, has done. Recently, military stalemate and the horror of war have brought renunciation of the absolutely exclusivist position and the proposal instead of "peaceful coexistence." This circumstance recalls the Treaty of Westphalia and the doctrine of *cujus regio ejus religio,* which brought an end to the religious wars in Europe.

The system's dynamism is such that, despite its short span of life, it now seems to be accepted as a governing system of values by as many people as accept Christianity. But despite Communism's vigor, the quasi-religious nationalist systems of Western civilization may be able to resist its expansion just as Islam and the ethnic religious systems of India and China have been able, by and large, to resist the spread of Christianity. The imperviousness of these religious systems to Christianity was particularly effective prior to 1750, when Oriental societies were still on a par with the Western Christian one in technological and economic terms.

Future Trends

As a reaction to secularist indifference and Communist disparagement, the traditional religions have tended to draw together recently.[14] With close contact among religious communities, there is a desire to eliminate friction. This is due both to a better understanding of other religious systems and to the shattering impact of the two world wars on religious thought, especially in the West. Since the 1893 meeting of the World Parliament of Religions in Chicago, various associations and unions, such as the World Congress of Faiths, have been set up to bring committed individuals from the traditional systems together in some

[14] See, e.g., Moses Jung *et al., Relations Among Religions Today* (Leiden: E. J. Brill, 1963).

sort of conversation. The aim of these conferences is to find areas of agreement, particularly on social and international political questions.

To some observers, these movements confirm the expectation of the nineteenth century Orientalist, Max Müller, that an elite group of followers of the different traditional religions would one day form the nucleus of a future church.[15] Some see pressures in the contemporary world leading to syncretistic efforts which will produce a new religion or modify an existing one by borrowing and incorporating the successful institutions and appeals of other systems.[16] Others, however, foresee a clinging to outworn religious symbols and a continuing pattern of co-existence among diverse confessions, rather than the evolution of a single world religion with a minimal or universal theology.[17] There remain, too, the religions and quasi religions which still aspire to become universal and perhaps expect to do so, their aspirations being muted only when the dialogue with other systems is under way.

Let us recall how religious systems have grown and spread. Religious struggles, marked by military conquests and forced conversions, have ended, not in Armageddon, but often in a stalemate of silent indifference. Is this the course to be followed by today's competing quasi-religious systems? At other times in the past, as at present, conditions have seemed ripe for a syncretism of valuable elements in the older religious systems, but could such a syncretism take hold today? A successful universalization of an ethnic religious system has occurred at least once before. One may wonder whether an American materialist quasi religion could become universalized by the selection of appropriate elements from the American ethos. Predictions about these and other alternatives may be more safely ventured when the ecological and spatial characteristics of contemporary religious systems have been analysed. To do so is one of the important tasks of the geography of religions.

[15] Friedrich Heiler, *Erscheinungsformen und Wesen der Religion,* Vol. 1 of *Die Religionen der Menschheit,* ed. C. M. Schröder (Stuttgart: W. Kohlhammer Verlag, 1961), p. 452.
[16] William Montgomery Watt, *Truth in the Religions: a Sociological and Psychological Approach* (Chicago: Aldine Publishing Company, 1963).
[17] Robert L. Slater, *World Religions and World Community* (New York: Columbia University Press, 1963).

index